Time for God

LESLIE D. WEATHERHEAD

ABINGDON • Nashville

Dedicated
to
ALICE M. HEAD

A small token of gratitude for
her friendship and encouragement
during thirty years

Time for God

A Festival Book

Copyright © 1967 Leslie D. Weatherhead
All rights reserved
Festival edition published May 1981
ISBN 0-687-42113-6

CONTENTS

THE THINGS WHICH REMAIN

PREFACE

I THOUGHT of calling this book, "To Start you Thinking", because I hope that these short sermonettes may usefully be the starting point for the discussion of groups, or what John Wesley called, "class meetings".

These little essays originally appeared in *The Sunday Times*, and I am grateful to the Editor for permission to publish them in this form. They were spread over a period of six years, and did not originally appear in the order followed here. Therefore some ideas are repeated which originally were separated by years. I am also grateful to Dr. Cecil Northcott, Editor of *The Lutterworth Press*, and to his staff for the help they have given me in compiling this book.

I must express gratitude also to my wife who has vetted no less than thirty-three earlier books and given me the benefit of her advice and judgment. My secretary, Miss Elsie B. Thompson, has helped me again with proof reading and with the many laborious tasks involved in preparing a book for the Press. I am very grateful to her.

Most of us have little time for reading and little inclination to read religious books, but perhaps on a Sunday morning, or as the starting point of a discussion, or for an invalid who wants quietly to meditate, these little essays may gently stimulate the mind.

If religion matters, and to my mind it matters as food and fresh air matter, then, however briefly, we must make time for God.

LESLIE D. WEATHERHEAD

Bexhill-on-Sea
Sussex.

THE INVIOLATE SOUL

The Quiet Heart

RECENTLY the stresses of life and the upheaval of change made me turn back to the life of Christ and read part of it again in our earliest gospel, that of St. Mark. It is hard to realize that Jesus Christ was one of the busiest men who ever lived. The things He got through in a day leave most of us standing—as we say. St. Mark's use of a word translated "straightway" seems to indicate the tumultuous demands made upon Him and the pressure of events upon His peace.

Yet never once do we get the impression of a person who has become hectic, impatient, irritable. He seemed to have had time for those who really needed Him. He spent half the night with a real seeker, and gave up His noontide siesta to talk with a woman by a well. There seems always to have been a poise of spirit, a quiet heart, an inward peace. So far from depending on others He was a refuge for every hunted spirit and brought the peace of God to every harassed mind.

WHAT was His secret? I can only think that He lived so near to God that He knew what God wanted Him to do at any one time. At any moment He knew what the will of God was for Him in the circumstances in which He found Himself. "In Thy will is our peace," said Dante. He moved from task to task, always within God's will.

Even ordinary people like ourselves can follow here. If we let the demands of tomorrow and the next day loom up too distressingly, as we tend to do about three o'clock in the morning after a sleepless night, if we let the pressure of the demands made on us overwhelm us, we can lose our peace. If, on the other hand, we can live a day at a time, saying, "This is what God wants me to do *now* anyway, and when I've done that I'll know what to do next,"—then we can often keep a quiet heart, quiet enough even to help another along the rough road of life.

"EVERY man can get through till nightfall," said the brave R.L.S. "Live in day-tight compartments," Sir William Osler advised his students, "tomorrow is another day." "As thy day, so shall thy strength be," says the old Book. Best of all are the words of the greatest Master of the art of living: "Don't fret about tomorrow. Tomorrow will take care of itself. Today's cares are quite enough for today." Exactly! I can't get tomorrow's strength until tomorrow. Why should I try today to carry tomorrow's burdens?

Mental Anchorage

WE LIVE in a troubled, unhappy, frightened world, and desperately need some true, rocklike idea to which our minds can anchor and on which they can rest. We must either stop thinking, or else stop and think.

It seems that many try the first alternative, filling every moment with the pursuit of pleasure and hobbies and work, or, if they are young, with wild adventure, and even violence, in order that they may not have to face the bogy of their own fears in a fear-stricken world.

Many try to think their way through, but they meet with continual disappointment. Nature says nothing to a frightened spirit, and science can frighten it still more. History from our small perspective shows little of a Divine Controller of events. Life in our perspective looks more like a confused tangle than a pattern.

MEN feel that the Church ought to have the answer, but they have grown tired of the disappointment that follows attendance at most services. Sporadically they pray, but it mostly seems like talking to nothing, and men become weary and give it up.

Always, in our search for a working philosophy of life, we must be ready to accept truth as soon as it authenticates itself in the mind, but in the meantime there is an anchor. It is the conviction that behind all things is Love.

Whenever we do a loving thing, we know it is a *good* thing to do. Love is the highest thing we know. It is incredible then that God is less than love, for that would make Him less than ourselves.

I AGREE that I cannot, in many situations, *perceive* that love is at work any more than a five-year-old son of a surgeon could think it "loving" to make a man unconscious and then cut him with knives!

The proof of love is not in the laboratory or the logic class. Love is only *proved* by commitment in faith to a loved person. To this commitment religion invites a man. Such commitment steadies the mind in a mad world. It is the only anchor I know.

"Don't Worry"

As one prone to worry, who hates the patronizing superiority of those with nothing to worry about who slap one on the back and say, "Don't worry", I should like to pass on a few hints about worry which I have found useful. Christ's words, "Take no thought", and "Be not anxious", mean "Don't worry", and they come from One who had everything to make Him worry, so we listen respectfully, but we may still wonder what to do about it.

Worry is the fruitless activity of a mind without issue in action. It is like racing the engine of a car. One uses petrol, but makes no progress. One wise tip, therefore, is to DO anything that can usefully be done. Instead of worrying half the night about a letter you have to write, sit up in bed and write it in rough. This, like letting in the clutch, turns fruitless activity into useful action. If nothing can yet be done, I find it helpful to *decide* what to do. If this happens I will *do* that. If that happens I will *do* this. Lin Yutang, the Chinese philosopher, said, "True peace of mind comes from accepting the worst." What actually happens is nearly always better than the worst we have imaginatively faced, and definitely deciding what we will do if . . . is a form of action.

We all know the parable of the little boy who fled from a witch who had turned herself into a pursuing cat. As the boy fled, and glanced fearfully over his shoulder, the cat grew to the size of a calf and then to the dimensions of an elephant. The boy fell, unable to go farther. Then he got up and faced the pursuing horror. As he advanced toward it, it diminished in size and retreated from him. Finally it changed into a mouse and ran under the door of the witch's cottage to be seen no more. What a parable of some worries!

PEOPLE say to the worrier, "Put it out of your mind!" No! Put it in the centre of your mind! Confront it! Decide what to do if even the worst happens, and summon all your powers to face it! Jesus said, "Don't worry because your Father knoweth". (Matthew 6: 32) When we've faced our worry and decided what to do, *then* we can put it out of our minds without its suppurating. We can turn then to our tasks, and the cleansed mind can rest on the strength of God, the God who can deal with every worrying situation and who always knows a way through.

Spiritual Catharsis

GEORGE ELIOT has somewhere the most attractive definition of a friend. I believe originally the definition stems from Arab sources. Anyway, here it is. "A friend is one to whom one can pour out all the content of one's heart, chaff and grain together, knowing that the gentlest of hands will take and sift it, keep what is worth keeping, and, with the breath of kindness, blow the rest away."

That is not the only function of a friend, but it is one of the most valuable, and the readiness of husband or wife to be a safety-valve for the other's pent-up feeling is one of the richest things in marriage. In a thousand domestic situations

15

wives would find immense emotional relief by "tipping out" the irritations of the day to husbands; and husbands who deceive themselves by supposing that they must keep their business and professional troubles to themselves would be amazed, delighted and refreshed in mind to find how readily a sympathetic and intelligent woman can grasp a business situation and ease a chafed mind by the simple process of listening. Besides, a wife is flattered by the desire of her husband to confide in her.

To go about telling everybody our troubles, discussing endlessly our symptoms, is the quickest way to lose friends. But there should be one or two close and wise friends with whom we can share.

One branch of the Christian Church specializes in the "Confessional". Like many other "means of grace" it can be misused. But it can be of enormous value to "exteriorize one's rottenness", as William James called it, in the ear of one who is trained to listen, who can advise, and who in the name of God will declare the divine forgiveness.

However, it is not just sin that we need to confess. People do not seem to realize that all ministers of the Free and Anglican Churches are trained to listen, to understand, to sympathize, to help, *and to keep confidences inviolate*. People should use the ministries of the Church to get the healing that comes from sharing their troubles with a discreet listener. Our sorrows, fears, worries, anxieties, forebodings and doubts become far less grim monsters when we have shared them with an adequate friend.

> Give sorrow words: the grief that does not speak,
> Whispers the o'er fraught heart and bids it break.

But we do not need the authority of Shakespeare. Everyone

knows that "a sorrow shared is a sorrow halved". Nor do we need a priest. Physical catharsis we all resort to occasionally. There is such a thing as mental and spiritual catharsis. That is where a true, wise friend comes in.

Why Did It Happen to Me?

Everyone asks this question when calamity falls. Few ask it when a joyous thing happens. Rarely can one find a causal connection either way. One's own folly, ignorance or sin may occasionally have brought one's troubles on oneself. In these days one suspects that one's worry, resentment, bitterness, jealousy, guilt or some other unhealthy emotion, long imprisoned in the deep mind, may have led to dis-ease of body or mind. Sometimes the causal connection is one's sin.

More frequently no such causal connection can be established, and it is morbid to lash one's memory and torment one's conscience by endlessly asking, "What have I done to deserve this?" In many ways life is like a game of football. In the clash of bodies *someone* is going to get hurt. The goal-keeper may never have to save a goal. On the other hand he may get a dislocated shoulder. He does not say, either about immunity or accident, "Why did this happen to me?" He says, "*We* lost", or "*We* won the game", and he takes the risk of personal injury. It's "all in the game".

In the clash of minds and free-wills, since we are all in the team and all liable to mistakes, although we gain by the skill of others, we suffer from the ignorance, folly and sin of others. In such a clash, *someone* is going to get hurt. Why not *us*? Our present disaster is our share in the team's strenuous effort. The Christian believes that in the end *the team* will win.

But the analogy does not go far enough. God has a concern for the individual. He *allows* things to happen that he does not *will*, just as a parent allows a little child to fall on the carpet, but not on the railway-line when a train is due. The very fact that a thing is allowed means that God can weave it into His overall plan. He would not allow a thing to happen which finally defeated His purpose. So the measure of our calamity must be the measure of our faith since this is the measure of God's weaving power, and what happens to us is less important than our reaction to what happens to us; a reaction which can help or hinder God's weaving.

GOD will help us to react to disaster, not by rebellion, self-pity and despair, but by our own brave answer to the question, "What is God trying to say to me through this evil which has befallen me?" He can make the individual's share of the ignorance, folly and sin of the world to praise Him. Jesus found that secret and, at a time when He might well have asked, "Why should this happen to me?", He turned thorns into a crown and a cross into a throne.

Christian Confidence

A FRIEND of mine once persuaded three men to grip a dynamometer or gripping machine. Their utmost effort produced a reading on the dial of an average of 101 lb. Then he hypnotized them and whispered in their ear that they could no longer grip, that their power to grip had vanished. He urged them to try, but repeated, "You can't!" Their average grip fell to 29 lb. While they were still hypnotized he asserted that power had returned. "You can!" he said. "You can!" Their average grip rose to 142 lb.: more than they could manage in the normal conscious state.

We may be surprised to read that Paul, so humble that he said he felt unworthy to be called an apostle, should, even when in prison, declare, "I can do all things in Him that strengtheneth me." (Phil. 4: 13.) But the very assertion "I can", even more powerfully than "I will", releases energy into personality, and in modern language we could translate thus: "When I think of Him I feel I can cope with anything, because of the power He gives me." When our minds really accept the thought, "I can", we open the door to God. If we say, "I can't", we slam the door in God's face and block His energies as well as paralysing our own.

> Though deep in mire, wring not your hands and weep,
> God lends His arm to all who say, "I can",
> No shamefaced outcast ever sank so deep,
> But he may rise again and be a man.

But Paul's claim went further than his own resources. "I can" opened the door which "I can't" shuts, but it opened the door to an entering Christ. "In *Him* that strengtheneth me" . . . Let a parable make the point. Imagine a great orchestra with no one conducting. A violinist in it is playing his best. Then enters the conductor, a great master musician. As soon as he raises his baton an added power is given to the violinist. Note this! If the violinist, on seeing the music, had put down his instrument and said, "I can't play this," the entry of the master musician would have made no difference.

It was because the violinist used to the uttermost his own ability that the master could bring him to a point of triumph which, unaided, he could never have reached.

A HEADMASTER I knew used to put his little daughter on a window-ledge six feet from the ground and bid her jump. "I can't," she would cry, and then add, "I can if you will catch me." Standing below her on the lawn he would smile and say, "When you jump, my arms will be there."

Traitor doubts can defeat us all. But the Christian believes that he is not left to face his troubles alone; that, when he makes the leap of faith, everlasting arms assist him; that when he says, "I can", God can, and will, and *does*.

Loneliness

LONELINESS is to be differentiated from solitude. Solitude is geographical and periodically desirable. Loneliness is spiritual and undesirable. Christ sought solitude among the lonely hills, but longed for human companionship. He chose twelve men "that they might be with Him", and must often have been grieved by their failure to sustain Him. We hear Him sadly ask, "Will ye also go away?" and, "Could'st ye not watch with Me one hour?"

Loneliness is a disease in the original meaning of that word. It is dis-ease; something that should be dealt with and ended. Further, it is sometimes a killing disease, leading to fatal alcoholism or to suicide. Many people who live alone never feel lonely, yet many who live with others and in crowded cities know only too poignantly how this disease makes them miserable.

When we think of loneliness we usually think of the aged who live alone, but a child new at boarding-school, a youngster starting in business, or a Serviceman new to the barrack room, can be as lonely as a solitary old woman in a one-room flat.

There *is* an answer in religion as long as the religious folk do not merely hand out empty words. To tell a lonely person that God is with him, seems to me an empty thing to say. It only fills with meaning and value if *a human being* mediates the undoubted friendship of God.

FOUR steps suggest themselves to me as a treatment of one form of loneliness:

1. The lonely person must relentlessly ask himself if his loneliness is his own fault. We remember the description of a famous Edward: "Edward is a small island entirely surrounded by Edward"! If we have shut ourselves in, asking for pity instead of offering service, wanting to be loved and forgetting that *the only way* to be loved is to love, then we must do something about it.

2. There is bound to be *some* church in our neighbourhood containing loving people whose loving is far more important than their creed or denomination, and in that fellowship the lonely person could find approval, acceptance, and a sphere of service for others.

3. In that service, which may not be "church-work" in the usual sense of the term, but working at his job to please God, or running a home for God's purposes, the lonely person may truly feel that he is co-operating with God in a vast plan beyond his present conceiving, but a plan which lends importance and dignity to every day.

4. When each day contains a quest for an opportunity to help another, the very outgoing of the mind diminishes one's own loneliness, and if one is too old or ill to run the world's errands, one can always pray. The saints say that that is the highest activity of all, and links one with both men and God.

The Will of God

I WISH we could reserve those words for situations which we believe to be God's ideal intention. Then we should be delivered from the heresy, with which some still torture themselves, of calling things like cancer and polio, frustration and premature death, the will of God. God, the great, creative Artist, cannot intend imperfection in the created object.

If a man drops a baby out of a fifth-storey window on to a hard pavement, I suppose one *could* say it is God's will that the baby should be killed, or He would have made babies of something like indiarubber. But it was not God's *will* that the baby should so be dropped, so the baby's death is not His will in any true sense of the word.

WE ALL suffer through the human family's ignorance, folly or sin, as well as through our own. God's will is to replace ignorance with knowledge, folly with wisdom, and sin with holiness. So nothing that is the result of ignorance, folly or sin can truly be called God's will, for it is not His intention. We get a glimpse of the will of God when, in the Gospels, we watch Jesus, not telling people that their illnesses were

God's will, but healing them. When a poor woman who had suffered for eighteen years was brought to Him, He did not say it was God's will that she should suffer. He said it was the work of Satan. (Luke 13: 16.)

Granted that God's will is often temporarily defeated, yet the wonder of the truth is that He can make evil serve His final purposes, as the Psalmist declared. (76: 10.) Omnipotence does not mean that everything that happens is God's will. When we say, truly, that God is omnipotent we mean that He cannot *finally* be defeated.

THE Cross itself seems to me the ideal illustration. It was a dastardly crime. As Peter said, (Acts 2: 23) it was brought about by wicked men, and wicked men do not do the will of God. But God used it and wove it into His triumphant plan which we call the redemption of the world.

Many of us in a smaller measure suffer and call it our "cross", but let us do what Jesus did—so co-operate with God that *in the end* all that is now so hard to bear is woven into a pattern of spiritual triumph. Professor C. H. Dodd translates Romans 8: 28 thus: "With them that love Him, God co-operates in all things for good."

The Shadow of Influence

WHAT a solemn thought it is that every one of us exerts an influence on others either for good or ill! The impact of our personality on another either makes it easier or harder for that person to live the good life. No one is neutral. No one counts for nothing. There is no one who makes not the slightest difference to other lives. We are either on the side of God or of the Devil; either we support the forces that make for goodness in the world, or those which make for evil. We cannot escape from this situation any more than we can escape casting a shadow on a sunny day, and it is either a shadow of healing or a shadow of harm. God, looking at our lives, knows which it is.

Even now in India, a Brahmin will throw away his rice if the shadow of an outcaste falls across it. Conversely, I used to see Indian people manœuvre themselves so that Gandhi's shadow might fall upon them and bring them blessing. One is not surprised to read in the book of Acts (5: 15) that they carried the sick into the streets, "that, as Peter passed by, his shadow might overshadow some one of them." They believed that a good man cast a healing influence around him, and, in a spiritual sense, how right they were! As Phillips Brooks, the famous American preacher, once said, "No man or woman of the humblest sort can really be strong, gentle, pure and good, without the world being better for it, without someone being helped and comforted by the very existence of that goodness."

OF COURSE, only rarely shall we *know* that another has been helped. Two hundred years ago a Puritan doctor wrote a book and died without knowing whether its shadow was healing or not. He called it *The Bruised Reed*. Richard Baxter was converted by reading it and he wrote *A Call to the Unconverted*. That book converted Philip Doddridge who wrote *The Rise and Progress of Religion in the Soul*. William Wilberforce read it and, inspired by it, wrote *A Practical View of Christianity*. Thomas Chalmers read it and was so affected by it that the revival he started in consequence influenced the whole history of Scotland. When a pebble is dropped into a pond no one can prophesy where the ripples will cease. Do not say, "Ah, but I cannot write books like that." The influence of a book is easier to trace, but the influence of a life is just as powerful. You have been dropped into a business, an office, a home, a factory, a workshop. Ripples are inevitable. Do they harm or help?

I have read of a Valley of Roses so extensive that the air is heavy for miles with the perfume of the flowers. And he who passes through the valley finds that the scent hangs in his very clothing, so that, if he goes into a room full of folk at the end of his journey, they look at one another and smile. *They know where he has been.* In the earliest days of Christianity men knew why Christians exerted such a marvellous influence on others. They stated the secret in a single sentence: "They have been with Jesus."

Looking past the Label

IT IS inevitable that we should label people but it is often distressing to note the way we do it. A man may live an honourable life of probity and usefulness for half a century, but let him then slip into one act which is unworthy, and it is by that act that he will be remembered and labelled. A man may be ideal in the home as husband and father. He may for years conduct a business ably and impeccably. He may serve his fellows with unselfish devotion and be a pillar of his church. But let him make one slip, especially if it be a sexual slip, and it is by this that he will be labelled. "Oh yes," men say as they try to recall his name, "you mean the man who . . ."

We say that A is a snob, B a neurotic, C a flirt and D a gossip, and so on to the end of the alphabet, but each is far more than such a label suggests, and the only accurate label is "The Mixture".

Christ always saw past labels. He was not unrealistic. He never pretended. So far from making light of sin, we know that if we were in His presence we should all feel ashamed, even if He spoke no word of rebuke. He accepted the label that Mary Magdalene was a harlot and that other sins stained her life. ("Her sins *which are many* . . .") But He saw past the label and added the blessed words, "she loved much." Zacchaeus wore the label of a despicable little profiteer, but Jesus saw past that label and said, "He *also* is a son of Abraham." We speak glibly of "the dying thief", but Jesus was ready to meet him in Paradise.

JOHN WESLEY tells of a man whom he labelled "mean" because he had given but little to a philanthropy for which Wesley had pleaded. Wesley's indignation was such that he expressed his contempt. The man made a strange answer. "I know a man," he said, "who buys, at the week's beginning, a pennyworth of parsnips, and boils them in water, and all the week the parsnips are his food and the water his drink." "Who is the man?" asked Wesley. "I am," said the man. Wesley adds, "This he constantly did although he had £200 a year, that he might pay the debts he had contracted before his conversion."

Let us look past labels. So easily do we identify a man with what he does, though we never label ourselves on that basis. So easily do we judge by appearances or by another's gossip. So rarely do we know all that lies behind.

A stained and cracked block of marble labelled "useless" stood in a builder's yard. "Send it to my studio," said

Michelangelo. "There is an angel imprisoned in it and I can set it free." So God thinks of us. So love would make us regard our brothers. Disapproval imprisons the hidden angel. Love would set it free.

Unanswerable Argument

To me the unanswerable argument for Christianity is that if Christ is taken seriously He changes men's lives. Any relationship with a loved person, to whom one looks up, has far more power to lift one than has a set of rules or a code of ethics. The girl who hates housework, will, after marriage, delight in it. Love releases energy and interest previously untapped. And if humbly, by faith, we practise communion with the living and loving Christ, He can still do for us what He did for men and women in Galilee.

During the war I attended a luncheon to which our host had invited a selection of men who claimed that their special interest could transform society: an educationist, an economist, an endocrinologist, a physician, a sociologist, a psychologist and a politician. After lunch, we all briefly spoke.

All, I felt, were making a valuable contribution to human well-being. But none alone, or all together, so it seemed to me, could achieve the maximum welfare of mankind. At each new stage of achievement, man's pride and selfishness prove to be the rocks on which the ship which sought Arcadia founders and sinks.

It is often forgotten how much our civilization owes to religion. The first schools were Church schools. The first hospitals in this country meaningfully bore the names of

27

saints. Justice was dispensed in churches, and the first "bar" to which barristers were called was the altar rail. The first plays in Britain were acted in church. The greatest artists painted sacred subjects, and great musicians like Handel chose accompanying words from the Bible.

I think it is not an unfair parable to say that the engine which gave the coaches of our culture their initial impetus has been detached, and though movement continues, as it does when a train is shunted and the engine uncoupled, one does wonder whether the train will arrive at a worthwhile station. Fourteen of the twenty-one civilizations this planet has known, says Toynbee the historian, have perished. They were instruments which God could no longer use.

When an American airman was shot down in the sea, taken to a Pacific island, formerly cannibal, and nursed back to health, he found himself in a community in which there was no murder, no drunkenness, no divorce, no poverty and no V.D. He asked the Chief the secret of all this happiness and well-being. The Chief looked at him reproachfully. "Your grandfathers taught us Christianity," he said simply, and then added, "We have taken Christ seriously." It is still open to us to do the same.

False Merit

WITHOUT doubt, the first law of mental serenity is that we should be utterly honest with ourselves. Yet how many of us live behind a facade of false merit where we carry on a hidden life full of the fear of discovery? Indeed, one only has to do that long enough to be deceived oneself by the facade, and to become not only unwilling but unable to see oneself as one really is. Introspection *can* become a morbid symptom of emotional disease, but, for most of us, a healthy hour of honest self-examination, followed by an acceptance of ourselves as we really are and a determination to do better, would be well spent.

Most of us meet criticism at some time or another. Here is our opportunity for honest self-examination. Are we really what the critic says? If so, let us be grateful for the revelation and put matters right. If not, the criticism can be discarded, but let us not pretend or hide from the truth. We sometimes pray in church that we may be "saved from our enemies and from the hands of all that hate us", but I have learnt far more about myself from my enemies than from my friends. The latter are sure to defend us, whatever we do or say, and they *can* anaesthetize our consciences by their kindness.

Further, in our quest for honesty, let us not assume false merit for what God has given us or for the opportunities men have made for us. It is laughable to watch a beautiful woman behave as though her beauty had been achieved. (Part of it has, I know!) The high-born often act towards the lowly as though *achievement* had brought them eminence.

Even academic distinction is usually the result of opportunity. Many humble working people known to me could easily have taken high university degrees if they had had the opportunity. And isn't it infuriating, if you are ill in bed, to have someone in robust and rude health standing pityingly over you as if his health were his own achievement and your illness your own fault?

Said Amiel, "We like to think of what has been given as having been acquired, and our lot in life as our conquest—an illusion born of vanity."

A Sufferer's Philosophy

A DOCTOR challenged me one day that the churches had never worked out a philosophy of life which would sustain a sufferer. I am sure this has often been done, but I will summarize my own point of view.

1. The will of God is perfect health of body, mind and spirit for all His children. No artist could *desire* imperfection in the created object.

2. Through the ignorance, folly or sin of the sufferer or, what is more likely, a member of the human family to which he belongs, the individual may suffer.

3. God is always eager to restore to health, but He has ordained that He will do so usually in co-operation with man. Otherwise divine omnipotence would abolish man's understanding and skill.

4. Those seeking to heal should ask and answer the all-important question: "How can we best co-operate with God—from whom alone all healing derives—in the case of this person?" The answer may be surgery, medical treatment, psychiatry, prayer, or the little known radiaesthetic energy or "odic force" which men like Mr. Harry Edwards possess. *Not one of these is a cure-all.*

Prayer may comfort and sustain, and even make illness seem unimportant, but God does not allow man, by putting a prayer in the slot and drawing out a cure, to escape the burden of research, skill and hard endeavour.

5. If a patient is healed, the will of God is done—though some hymns about "Thy will be done" would suggest the

opposite. If the patient is unhealed, God is only *temporarily* defeated. The triumphant fact about religion and suffering is that God can weave into His ultimate plan whatever happens to us, and bring us to *His* goal even though ours is never reached. If the Cross, devised by evil men, could be turned into a victory which redeems the world, then even cancer, whatever its cause, cannot finally defeat God's plan in the life of any of His children.

6. Suffering has no power to make a saint, but courage, faith and prayer can help the patient to make such a reaction to suffering as to turn liability into asset.

7. Let us never look on suffering and say, "This is the will of God", since a *man* who deliberately thus wrought his will would be sent to prison or a mental hospital. Let us labour to end the causes of suffering, and to help God weave what we cannot remedy yet into spiritual victory, as Christ did when He accepted the Cross.

Make Up Your Mind!

I WISH I could write some sentences to persuade some reader who has never made up his mind about the Christian religion to do so. There are so many splendid people among one's friends and acquaintances who would never act dishonourably or meanly, who are full of generosity and helpfulness if ever one is in trouble or need, and yet who withhold their allegiance from any denomination of the Church or any outward expression of religious faith.

Many feel that the church services are dull, boring and irrelevant. Many have been put off by the frailties of church members. Many men, I am sure, hate hypocrisy more than anything, and, rather than fall below the profession of being a Christian which going to church involves, they will profess nothing and be "better than their creed". Many wives are unwilling alone to join the fellowship of the Church. Many, both husbands and wives, no longer believe the creeds of the Church and feel that their intellectual integrity would be impugned by association with the Church. Indeed, many professing atheists are nearer belief in the true God than are many conventional churchgoers who believe in a bogy that does not exist and whom they miscall God.

For these, and a hundred other reasons, some of the grandest people I know stand on the touchline instead of playing in the team to which they could contribute so richly in thought, experience of life, service to others and example. It looks as if they will do this until the whistle blows.

Clearly the Church must take much of the blame. If we had spoken of God more winsomely and adequately, and revealed in our lives a more attractive quality of life, men and women would not have been put off the grandest thing in the world. But how much finer it would be if those who criticize—even justly—would join in with us so that they could help make the Church what they feel it ought to be.

Surely there is *some* church in *some* denomination which would meet their need—for they have needs—and through which they could serve the present age which so desperately needs what they can *give*. It is only in fellowship with others that we truly find ourselves, and are released to the point of that self-giving which enriches others also.

Belonging to the Church is not believing a hundred theological propositions. It is rather, in fellowship with

Christ and others who love Him, to react to all life's challenges in His spirit and to try to extend His Kingdom, which is the Kingdom of right relationships, with God and with all mankind.

Make up your mind! Conflict and indecision in the mind are always exhausting, and it is very feeble and unsatisfactory to dilly-dally in a matter of such tremendous importance.

It May Be Later than You Think

IT IS sometimes good to recall our New Year resolutions, if we made any; for they have a queer way of losing any urgency which the turn of the year gave them. Unfortunately, as most of us discover, changing from one year to the next effects in itself no change in our natures, and unless we take ourselves in hand with determination the new year will be only a dreary repetition of the faults and failings of the old. All that is different, beside the date, is an added ounce of cynicism which makes us decide that we are what we are and that nothing has power to change either us or anyone else.

THE figures which pull me up more than the change in date are as follows. Reduce a lifetime of seventy years to the compass of the waking hours of a single day, say, from 7 a.m. until 11 p.m. Then if your age is

15	the time is	10.25 a.m.	35	the time is	3.00 p.m.
20	,, ,,	,, 11.34 a.m.	40	,, ,,	,, 4.08 p.m.
25	,, ,,	,, 12.42 p.m.	45	,, ,,	,, 5.16 p.m.
30	,, ,,	,, 1.51 p.m.	50	,, ,,	,, 6.25 p.m.

55 the time is 7.34 p.m.	65 the time is 9.51 p.m.
60 ,, ,, ,, 8.42 p.m.	70 ,, ,, ,, 11.00 p.m.

"Swift to its close ebbs out life's little day." And what after that? Christians believe that there follows a life which spiritually goes on where this life left off and which bears a definite relation to the way this life was lived.

IF MAN really is essentially a spiritual being, any capacity other than a capacity to enjoy spiritual things will fall away useless, though the word "spiritual" is bigger than orthodox religion dreams.

When a beloved daughter asked her dying father if she should read the Bible to him, the old Scottish saint replied: "Nay, lassie, it's ower late the noo. I theekit [thatched] ma hoose before the storm started."

Blessed is he who, in our Lord's phrase, has "treasure in heaven". Perhaps a wise proverb for all of us is this: "Hurry up! It may be later than you think."

The Church's Obsession with Sin

No SERIOUS Christian dare make light of sin. It hurts the sinner and it hinders God. In my opinion, however, the Church has for centuries painted so dark a picture of sin and its consequences that men whom Divine forgiveness should have set free, never escape the sense of being guilty sinners.

This stems back to Paul, not to Jesus. Jesus is reported as using the noun for "sin" on only six occasions and the verb on only three. Paul uses them ninety-one times. Jesus forgave men freely. Paul, with his Jewish background and legal training, seems to have an obsession about sin and guilt, and he sees the Cross as the climax of Jewish sacrifices, and Jesus as a Lamb slain to "satisfy" or "make expiation" or "propitiation"; words which seem to deny the readiness of any father to forgive, without some innocent person "paying the price of sin" or suffering in the sinner's stead.

The Anglican Prayer Book, in spite of much lovely English, makes the picture darker still, and one feels sorry for the "Anglican" who only goes to church for weddings, baptisms and funerals. He is told that his marriage is "a remedy against sin and to prevent fornication". When he brings his baby for baptism he finds the magic hasn't worked, for the very first prayer is one for deliverance from God's wrath—against a tiny baby! The second prayer asks for the remission of the baby's sins, though he is generally about a month old! Finally, it is prayed that "all carnal affections may die in him" forgetting that without "carnal affections" he would not have been born, and that if the prayer is answered, his wife-to-be will have a thin time! At every funeral there is talk about God's "wrathful indignation" and "displeasure" at our sins. Poor Cranmer is mainly responsible for most of this, and we know that his sadistic schoolmaster gave him an obsession about guilt and sin, but it is time the Church escaped from it.

What a corrective to our gloom about sin it would be to realize that Christ's story of the prodigal's return did not end even in a prayer-meeting, let alone punishment, but in roast veal and a dance!

Dread of Disapproval

LETTERS about my article called "The Church's Obsession with Sin" make me want to fight the fear of disapproval which drives so many from Church, or from consulting, in times of trouble, the clergy and ministers of religion. People seem quite surprised and delighted if the latter appear "human" and able to understand them. Their ministerial training and work ought to make them the most understanding of all men, yet young people in trouble fear the wagging finger of disapproval, and older people often refrain from attending Holy Communion because they feel "unworthy".

How completely Christ would sweep away that barrier! If He disapproved of what people *did*, His love, and His belief in them as persons of infinite worth to God, would get across to them and sustain them.

I love the interruption the father makes in the story of the Prodigal. (Luke 15: 22) The son intends to say: "Make me as one of your paid servants." But the father never lets him get as far as that. With a glorious interruption, he flings his arms round the boy (N.E.B.), and calls for all the symbols of sonship: robe, shoes, and even the ring with its seal of authority.

If we were to go to the Master, ready to confess everything, and even wallow in morbid and self-despising guilt, He would, I feel, interrupt and say: "Yes, I know, but now we are united all that is over." His love and belief in us would create new life within us and re-create our self-respect.

The Church has always been afraid of being as loving as its Master. We just cannot really believe that "this Man receiveth sinners". Still less can we really believe that He is the "friend of sinners", and, on His own word, loves them as much as He loves the saints. God's love, He told us, falls as impartially as the rain, and shines with no more favouritism than the sunrise (Matthew 5: 45). How many of us need just that! Instead of feeling disapproved of, to feel loved, believed in, and accepted. The mind needs approval as the body needs food and fresh air.

I once had an Airedale dog, a constant and lovable companion. He had a real sense of sin! If he had stolen, or attacked a cat, or killed a hen, my reproving voice made his tail drag, and his eyes grow mournful. But the pat of restoration and forgiveness made him race round the garden in an ecstasy of joy.

I wish I could convey to those who listen to my preaching the tremendous joy that could be theirs by one simple act of the acceptance of God's loving forgiveness. To be one with God means restored peace of mind, and often restored health of body. Charles Wesley wrote, "My heart it doth dance at the sound of His Name!" So it could be for us.

The Wrath of God

CORRESPONDENTS have accused me of minimizing "the wrath of God". It is an unfortunate phrase, and far too anthropomorphic to be true of God. It suggests the kind of anger which expresses itself in reprisals. One remembers "incurring the wrath" of a schoolmaster! The Bible may say, "a soft answer turneth away wrath", but at my school a soft answer turned it on! Our human passions can have no exact equivalent in a perfect Being.

If a bully robs an old woman of her life-savings, or a drunkard rapes a child, of course we feel wrathful, and surely God cannot be impassive. Indeed, our dirty little sins must be blacker against His whiteness than sordid crime is to us.

Even so, Jesus taught us to love the sinner even while we hate his sin. This seemed a quibble to me until I realized that I never identified my own sins with myself! "I can't think what possessed me to do such a thing," we say. And, while hating our sin, we go on believing in ourselves, and indeed, loving ourselves. Jesus underlined that we must love our neighbour as ourselves.

Some of my correspondents seem terribly anxious that God should punish the wicked! Possibly their own insecurity motivates this attitude, and they feel that virtue will be more richly rewarded if the wicked are damned! Why, they might as well have had "a good time" themselves! They secretly feel that the wicked have more fun than the good, reminding me of the curate who, asked if he had enjoyed Paris, said, "Yes, but I wish I had visited it before I was converted."

I would define "the wrath of God" as His anger against those forces which lure men with false rewards and lead them down paths which only end in frustration, disillusionment and grief. So a man might hate the cancer which is eating away the fair body of his beloved, and who hates it the more because he loves her so much. His wrath is an expression of his love. So is "the wrath of God".

God hates evil because it deprives man of the highest joy of which he is capable and the fullness of life for which he was designed. But His attitude to the sinner is unvarying love and compassion, a longing that he may "turn from his wickedness and *live*".

When I Am Afraid

WE NEED not be ashamed of being afraid. Fear is universal. The man who "does not know what fear is" is a myth. If he existed, he could not know what courage was, either. For courage is the determination to overcome fear by facing the fear-causing situation and wresting from it personal triumph. There is enough happening in the world, let alone our private lives, to cause fear. The important thing is to react to it usefully.

If our fears have no discernible basis in reason—like those spasms of panic which we know at 3 a.m. or on waking— we must either see a psychiatrist or learn to dismiss them. To dwell on them is only to increase their power over us.

The Psalmist says, "What time I am afraid, I will trust in Thee." (Psalm 56: 3.) It is good advice as long as by "trust" we do not mean an expectation that God will alter the fear-causing situation. This would make religion an insurance scheme against disaster and men would try to pay the premium with a spurious piety. Immunity is nowhere promised in the Gospels. Jesus did not promise His men an escape from those evils which are the common lot of us all. Indeed, He told them that just because they were His they would meet added danger and persecution. But He did promise that He would be with them, and see them through, and that no evil power could finally snatch them out of

His hand. The word "omnipotence" never means that God will do everything we want, or that everything that happens is His will. It means that nothing that happens ever defeats Him finally.

THE story of the storm on the lake (Mark 4: 36) has been grievously misunderstood. When Jesus said, "Peace, be still," He was talking to the men, not to the waves. Storms on Galilee still suddenly rise and as suddenly subside. But men who spread fear by crying out need to be silenced. Afterwards, all those men met far more terrible deaths than drowning. No Divine power intervened. But by then they had realized that everlasting arms are round all souls, whatever happens to bodies, and that neither accident, nor disease, nor any kind of evil can prevent those who trust Love from arriving—on this side of death or the other—at their appointed goal.

The Inviolate Soul

A MAN wrote to me recently, troubled because his wife had been persuaded to undergo an operation which, he said, had changed her character. "It worries me," he said, "that the *self* can be changed, and her way of looking at things altered, by surgery or even by drugs." People whose relatives suffer from mental illness worry similarly: "Is the innermost *self* mad?"

Here is a parable. Imagine a man locked in a room with crinkly glass in its only window. He, looking out, sees a distorted world. Others, looking in, see a distorted person.

But the cause of the distortion is the window, not the person. Similarly, after certain treatments, surgical or sedative, or in certain conditions, mental or emotional, the patient seems to his friends abnormal, and the world seems different to him. But the cause of the distortion is the condition of brain and nerve and disturbed feeling which separate the real self of the patient from his world and his friends. *He* himself, his soul, is as untouched as the man in our parable is unaffected by the glass through which he looks out and others look in.

Here is another relevant parable: Imagine a man whose only means of communicating with others is by playing his violin. If his violin is taken away and smashed, he is still a violinist. He still loves music. His ability is not destroyed. *No one can touch that.* "Fear not them that kill the body," said Jesus, "and after that have no more that they can do." (Luke 12: 4) The soul is inviolate and goes on into another phase of being, picks up another instrument, which Paul called "the spiritual body" (1 Corinthians 15: 44) and plays even more glorious music than the physical body and brain could express.

Death, disease, mental disharmony and emotional disturbance may affect the body, the brain and the senses which depend on it. But all these were only instruments which the soul used on this plane of being. The inviolate soul will not have suffered deprivation, let alone annihilation. God has had access to the soul all the time.

To those whose loved ones are dead, or mentally ill, or physically worn out, or ravaged with disease, I would say, "Be of good cheer! The soul is inviolate. It dwells in the innermost sanctuary of being. God keeps its key on *His* girdle, and none may enter but He."

The Providence of God

CAN man believe today in an overwatching Providence that cares and guides? It would be easy to argue, "No!" War, disease, hunger, poverty, calamity and accident blight men's lives and ruin their happiness. God may be both powerful and loving, but He rarely seems to *act*, and prayer seems so often a fatuous waste of time.

For myself, I cannot believe in what has been called a "special providence". The selfish piety which sees deliverance from the calamities which fall upon others as a sign of divine favour to oneself, seems to me bad theology and spiritual conceit. In many situations it is mentally healthier to believe in sheer good luck.

Further, to equate providential care with unearned privileges, material security or physical health seems to me a delusion.

The splendid lives of so many who lack nearly "all the blessings of this life" cry to high heaven against such a heresy. Certainly no faith in God's providence could be based on it.

We must be careful not to call the will of God those distressing happenings which are simply due to the fact that we are members of the human family. We gain from the family wisdom and achievement, though we do not deserve to do so, as individuals. We suffer from the family ignorance, folly and sin, without any personal deserving.

MY OWN faith is that God is not only interested in, but

implicated in every life, and is working purposefully within it. Both His love and power are shown, not in preventing what we call evil, but in co-operating with us to weave everything that happens into a pattern which at last will turn out to be more wonderful and beautiful than we can now foresee.

Therefore, not what happens to us, but our reaction to what happens to us is the important factor. Our resentment, rebellion, self-pity and other negative reactions can hinder His weaving and our own spiritual, mental and physical health. But to say in our sorrow, "What is God trying to say to me in this situation which has befallen me?" and to meet it with cheerful and courageous co-operation, is to compel it to enrich us. Such a reaction is difficult to make. Even Christ shrank from the Cross. But if we try to make it, we shall reach a peak from which, *looking back*, we shall see that all along a Hand guided and a Heart cared. God was with us when we knew it not, and what His Providence provided was His own unbreakable love and a creative possibility in every event.

Peace of Mind

PERHAPS the quality most to be desired in these days is peace of mind. The sale of tranquillizers is an indication of our modern quest for it. In one year, through the National Health Service, 350 million sleeping tablets and 2,000 million aspirins were obtained by the patients of Britain! Britain is the most comfortable country in Europe. It also has the highest suicide rate. I was told in America that one in twelve of the entire population spends some time in a

43

mental hospital. Inquiries here showed the proportion to be one in fifteen; high enough for concern.

Some seek mental peace in holidaying as often as possible, in hobbies, in alcohol, in pep-pills, in dance halls, or watching "telly", in frantic efforts never to be alone, never to be quiet, always to be entertained.

IT IS not very helpful to list the causes of our unrest. The hectic pace of life, anxiety about security, about health, business worries, a feverish quest for unsatisfying goals, the noise, rush and speed of modern traffic and always the background fear of atomic war add up to more than the unaided nerves can stand. Can the Christian religion help? I think inward peace could be maintained if we could do six things:

1. If we could get rid of the sense of guilt by accepting God's forgiveness and starting again, even if it is the thousandth new beginning.

2. If we could put things right with any person in the world with whom we are wrong, even if we have to climb down, lose face, ask pardon, and make restitution.

3. If we could aim to live each day within the will of God as we perceive it at each decision, remembering Dante's famous words: "In Thy will is our peace", this would keep our sense of values straight.

4. If we could make a tiny place each day, however short, for meditative prayer. Ten minutes in a church on the way to work, or out of the dinner-hour, or on the way home, would work a miracle of peace.

5. If we could live a day at a time, instead of endlessly saying: "Whatever shall I do if . . ." We are to plan ahead with as much wisdom as we can contrive, but in the business of living surely we are to withdraw our attention from everything but the task in hand.

6. If we could rest our minds in the thought of God's omnipotent purposefulness. His omnipotence does not mean that everything that happens is His will. Nor does it mean that He will interfere with overwhelming might. It means that He cannot be defeated ultimately in His purposes. And He has a purpose for every life.

When we read the Gospels, we do not always realize how busy Jesus was and what He got through in a day. Yet this busy Man only left one thing in His will. "My peace I leave with you." Can we fulfil the conditions by which we can lay hold on our promised inheritance? It is worth trying.

Christianity Means Joy

JESUS seemed so eager that men should be joyous. He wanted them to have His joy and that their own should be "filled to the full". "Be of good cheer!" seems to have been a sentence continually on His lips, and surely no other religious teacher has ever described himself as a Bridegroom, or fellowship with Him as a continuous wedding feast. (Matthew 9: 15)

What a pity, then, that so many of His followers give the impression of being at a continuous funeral! The will of God is joy for all His children, yet the very phrase has been often used to describe only what is melancholy and sad.

Of course, no mind can unceasingly express any emotion, even joy, but though hot circumstance may dry up the stream of gladness trickling down the mountain side of experience, the deep lake above, which feeds it, never dries up. Our smiles may evaporate in times of trouble, but the deep reservoir of Christian joy none can take from us. Indeed, the opposite of joy is not sorrow. The opposite of joy is unbelief.

The New Testament contains enough tragedy to make it the saddest book in the world, but it opens with the songs of angels bringing "tidings of great joy", and it closes with the Hallelujah Chorus sung by all the ransomed hosts of heaven. One of its greatest figures, Paul, even when in prison, shouts to his followers, "Rejoice in the Lord always. Again I say it, Rejoice!" "Joy is the flag which flies from the castle of the unconquered heart because the King is in residence."

Today there is enough to make us sorrowful, but the Christian message is a gospel. The word means "Good news". Without Christ, gloom might conquer, but He has a reply to everything that makes us sad. For sin, forgiveness. For death, survival and reunion. For suffering, increasing victory and the final weaving into a joyous pattern of all our troubles. For evil, the promise of final triumph. For war, slums, hunger, poverty and vice, an increasing awakening and a growing determination to end them all.

Let us, then, play the glad game, advertise our religion by showing forth its assets; for the joyous, royal, radiant and victorious Christ is with us.

MOTIVES AND ENDS

Why Should We Worship God?

THEOLOGIANS tell us that God cannot *need* worship. He is all-sufficient and even the capacity to worship—which is a mark of the soul—is His gift. Yet I think worship must please Him, as it pleases me if a little child comes into my garden, plucks a flower which is mine already, and gives it to me. Whatever our worship may mean to *God* it does three important things for *us*.

1. Who has not heard the cry, "Switch the light on, I cannot see!" or, "Open the window, I cannot breathe"? When the minister says, "Let us worship God," the worshipper should realize that the service offered is the provision of the environment in which the soul of man can function. As the eye cries out for light, the lungs for air and the mind for truth, the soul cries out for God. Life is correspondence with the relevant environment. Worship provides the environment for the highest form of life of which man is capable.

2. The word "worship" comes from the same root as the words "worth", "worthy" and "worthwhile". When we worship God we admire in Him those qualities which are worthwhile. Drinkwater wrote, "Who worships greatness passing by, himself is great." When we admire God's holiness and love, then, to a tiny extent, we imbibe holiness

49

and love. We become like what we admire. Further, any emotion is strengthened by expressing it. (Kiss your wife and see!) And when, in a service, we sing, "Holy, holy, holy," though we ascribe the virtue to God, our expressed admiration of what is worthy and worthwhile increases the quality in ourselves.

3. A third value in worship is that it helps us get our sense of values right. A correspondent wrote to me, "Having been to your service this morning, I find I just cannot do the unworthy thing I had planned to do." The writer had been too near God! What a mess a shopkeeper would be in —to quote William Temple—if, unknown to him, someone changed the price labels on his goods! This has happened in our world.

Making money, having sex-fun, getting on, pleasure: these are valued highly. Humility, faithfulness, obligation, serving others—these are marked low and even despised. Worship helps us to enthrone a right sense of values.

When the *Titanic* went down, a wealthy woman took into the lifeboat, not her diamonds, but a bag of oranges. It will be very important, where we are going, that we value the right things. Worship often makes us examine our luggage.

The Modern Sunday

OUR thoughts about Sunday have vastly altered in the last fifty years, and the behaviour of many would suggest that there should be no criticism expressed by anyone on what is done on Sundays. Yet while we are glad that the ancient tyrannies have gone, I would like to make the plea that Sunday is worth saving, and to do so by means of a parable.

I know a little park with beautiful flower beds, well-cut lawns, shady trees, a rock garden and even a little pond. The park is locked at night. Iron railings surround it, and there are notices, "Do not pick the flowers," and in a few places, "Please keep off the grass." A critic might ask, "Why the notices, the palings, the locked gates?" But clearly the answer is that, without them there would soon be no park for anyone.

Sunday is a little park, an oasis in the desert of this noisy, hectic, rushing weekday life. If we do not guard and protect it, there will soon be no Sunday for anyone.

When Moses came down Mount Sinai armed with the rules which he believed would best safeguard the well-being of his people, he included this one: "Remember the sabbath day, to keep it holy". (Exodus 20: 8) The word "holy" could be translated "healthy" and the word "Sabbath" comes from an old Babylonian root meaning, "Stop doing what you normally do!" Blessed and wise is he who follows, even in modern days, the implications of those words. "The Sabbath was made for man," said Jesus. But a man is not just a clever animal, but a spirit clothed in a body and using a mind. His true health demands time and attention given to body, mind *and spirit*. Communion with God is as essential to the health of the spirit as communion with true ideas is essential to the health of the mind, and as communion with food and fresh air is essential to the body.

Did Christ Disapprove of Wealth?

THE answer to the question must be "No". Did He not praise the man who turned five talents into ten? Did He not accept without criticism the hospitality of rich men? Did He not wear such good clothes that those who crucified Him cast lots for them rather than cut them up? Did He not praise Abraham who was probably the richest man in the Bible?

No one could claim that Christ was wealthy, but He did not "wonder where the next meal was coming from", for Judas kept a bag and wealthy women kept the band in funds. (Luke 8: 3) When Jesus said He "had not where to lay His head", He meant that He must be continually on the move. Scores would have been proud to give Him accommodation, as the sisters in Bethany did.

He told the rich young ruler to "sell all that he had" because *in his case* wealth was a stumbling block. It would be foolish and indeed impossible to take one sentence spoken to one man in one special set of circumstances as if it applied to all men in all circumstances. Clearly if some Christian employers parted with all they had, they would put others for whom they are responsible out of work. Money honestly earned, generously used and invested to provide material security for loved ones can be a blessing.

But Jesus did say that to make money has its dangers. It is like exchanging my push-bike for a car. I can do far more good. I can give people lifts and can double my own mobility and halve my fatigue. But I am in greater danger.

I can hurt others and myself far more when I drive a car than when I ride a bike. So it is with money.

Let us list some of the dangers. Men are tempted to think that money will buy spiritual security. Those who feel no need of anything more easily feel no need of God. With money men patronize others and harm both themselves and those whose gratitude salves the consciences of the rich. Money can make us develop a wrong sense of values. Many a man who looked *through* glass and saw and heeded the needs of others, has, as it were, by making money, coated the glass with silver. Now he does not see the needs of others. He sees only himself. Silver ruined his vision.

If, at some point, we seem challenged with the words of the old highwayman, "Your money or your life," we must choose life. For Jesus did not say, "I am come that they might make money." He did say, "I am come that they might have life." But to the truly dedicated person his money is an extension of his personality and a spiritual, as well as a material, asset.

Symbol of Waste

EVERY reader of the Gospel loves the story in Mark 14: 3, of the woman who anointed Christ with expensive ointment. I must not take space here to expound this thrilling drama. Suffice it to say that her loving extravagance drew hostile criticism from the disciples, who murmured, "To what purpose is this waste?"

One of the hardest things to be decided by the thoughtful Christian is the allocation of his wealth. If the disciples could now see Coventry Cathedral, or the Pope's robes, or the City Temple organ, or my car, would they say: "To what purpose is this waste? This might have been sold for much and given to the poor. How can they spend like this when people are starving? Haven't they heard of Oxfam?"

Yet Jesus praised the woman's extravagance, even though He was reminded about the poor. "She has done a lovely thing to me," he said, "and her story shall be repeated wherever the gospel is preached." (Mark 14: 6 and 9.)

I HAVE no advice to give about the material priorities of the Christian. It is a very intimate matter and everyone must decide it for himself in the light of his commitments and concern, but we could usefully consider the waste of human lives. A woman whose son was killed in the last war wrote to me and said: "It is bad enough to lose a son, but to know that his life has been wasted is worse than death." But I do not believe it was wasted. Where would our country be today but for so-called "wasted lives" like his? I may listen to a speaker pleading the pacifist case in Hyde Park, but except for thousands who died in war the speaker would not have the freedom to denounce war!

Another letter sounds a different note. When a mother who similarly had lost her son was receiving sympathy she wrote: "Do not grieve for me. He had twenty years of happy life and then he died for England. What better thing could have happened?" This was no wasted life.

Whatever we do about our possessions, let us at least be clear about what we mean by a wasted life. I make no facile sneer about modern youth, for I am sure that if war broke out our young moderns would sacrifice themselves as readily as their fathers did, but when I see the long-haired youths and the screaming girls giggling away their days, and watch some adults who spend meaningless days in squeezing out of their dismal lives the last drop of pleasure for themselves, with never a thought of service or sacrifice, I am in no doubt about whose life is being wasted.

Which is the symbol of waste, the expensive jar of precious ointment sealed, neatly labelled and safe on some shelf, or a jar broken and its contents spilled, but with a fragrance released that fills the world and calls forth the praise of Christ?

Sex and the Soul's Health

Let the reader imagine that he is starving; that he is imprisoned, securely fastened in a chair, in a room in which there is neither sight nor smell of food; and that a succession of waiters pass through the room carrying trays on which he can see the most appetizing food. Here is an instinctive appetite not only denied fulfilment, but *aroused* and still denied. Then let the reader imagine that, when the last dish has disappeared, he is released from the chair and set free. Is there any doubt but that he would seek to allay his appetite, and would, after its titillated arousal, almost commit crime to get at food?

Sex is also an instinctive hunger. Christians believe that, so far from being wicked or beastly, it is part of the divine plan. It is no more "wicked" to long for sexual fulfilment and satisfaction than to be hungry at dinner-time. But he who steals food because he is hungry does a wrong to society, and if caught he is punished. And he who, because he is sexually hungry, steals an experience, also does a wrong to society and in the end is punished by his own loss of self-respect and by an ultimate guilt-distress not less painful because for many years it can be repressed, and can wait until late in life to exact its nemesis in terms of anxiety and depression.

Many people inside the framework of marriage satisfy completely and legitimately their sexual desires. But it should be remembered that thousands of young, healthy people and older, frustrated people cannot do this. If, in this state, they are sexually aroused, though they enjoy the arousal, the battle of self-control is made harder. Fantasies are made by the imagination in solitary hours, and in these fantasies the mind so revels in sex experiences that, should sudden temptation become actual, the battle, already yielded to by imaginative lusting, is lost because the mind moves along the road already prepared for it. The Romans could say all that in four words: *Cogitatio, imaginatio, delectatio, assensio.* ("I muse, and then let my imagination get to work until I delight in some sexual scene and finally I fall.")

He who, by literature or art, arouses passions and appetites which we cannot satisfy without hurting others or lowering our own ideals, who drives us, when we come to ourselves, into a kind of secret shame, is no friend of society. He provides the imagination with the poison that kills virtue. And poison is just as deadly when it is offered to us in a beautiful cut-glass decanter called literature. That is why books like *Lady Chatterley's Lover* should be left in obscurity by a nation trying to put first things first and concerned with the health of the soul.

A Family Affair

I HEARD a lady described recently as of "independent means". Apart from the people who get up and go out on bitter mornings to make her dividends, is she independent of the plumber? I'm not! Is she independent of the doctor, the butcher, the grocer, the milkman, the dustman? How she would scream if one of them "let her down"!

Let me illustrate further from the lady. She rose one winter morning to take a bath, the plumber having unfrozen the pipe and made that possible. A Frenchman handed her a cake of soap, a Pacific islander a sponge, and a Turk a towel. Her clothes involved a dozen others. At breakfast, a Chinese poured out her tea, a West Indian popped in the sugar, a farmer had been out in deep snow to get her milk and her eggs. The baker had been up long before she awakened to get her new rolls ready. A Spaniard passed her the marmalade and a Jamaican a banana.

A lady of independent means! She was dependent on people all over the world before she made up her idle mind whether to yawn at a matinée that afternoon or to play bridge. She is a parasite on society, taking from the family daily and giving nothing in return.

We simply must wake up to the fact that life is a family affair and we must all help. As St. Paul said, "We are members one of another." And the awakening becomes more urgent as the whole world becomes a neighbourhood.

I get on quite well with Aunt Agatha. She is admittedly difficult but she lives in Glasgow and I in the south. I send her a Christmas card and relationships are easy. If she came to live in our town it would be more difficult; if next door, much more difficult. If she came to live with us it would become a matter of urgency and primary importance to find a philosophy of life which provided a basis for getting on together.

Fifty years ago China was in another city. So were Africa and India and even the U.S.A. Now all the nations are next door neighbours and we are practically living together even with those who don't want us.

CHRISTIANS believe that their religion of brotherhood—sustained by a Father who loves and values all alike, whatever the colour of their skin or the development of their brains—provides the necessary basis for living together as a world family. In an ideal family, the assets of one are at the disposal of all; the needs of one challenge the resources of all; the sins or failures or weaknesses of one are the concern of all. Equality is not claimed, save equality of relationship.

No one who has belonged to a large family pretends that all are "equal". There are little brothers who are not allowed yet to keep a shot-gun, and are not asked to run a business. But no one is treated in an unbrotherly way and all are helped to grow up and make their contribution to family life. Not one is independent.

Policies which make life in this world a family affair will succeed. Policies, like apartheid, which divide men will fail. For a world-family is God's will. And it is *His* world.

Motives and Ends

A CORRESPONDENT asked me to write about motive, because he undertook a piece of work with what he calls a "sinful motive". He feels that, although the contemplated work is entirely above-board and of value, it is ruined by its motivation, and he wonders whether he ought to give it up.

I feel it important to point out in the first place that the value of a piece of work is to be assessed by the objective to which it is directed, and not by the nature of the impetus which caused it to be undertaken.

In the second place, it is important to realize that a single motive is exceedingly rare. There are nearly always several motives, even though some remain unconscious.

In the third place, instinctive urges, self, sex or social, are usually among the dynamic motives, but this does not invalidate the value of the work done in response to them, or make the motivation unworthy.

Dr. Hadfield, who taught me so much about motive, tells of a woman who devoted her life to rescuing "fallen girls", only to discover, during analysis, that her dynamic motive was sexual curiosity. She then felt she must give up her work. But if she had done so, sex curiosity would not have ceased to plague her, and might have found a less socially valuable outlet. Mental health lies in recognition of *all* our motives and directing them to an end which is of social value. It was sheer gain for her to recognize that the instinct which induced her to take up this kind of work was the

59

same as that which made the girls "fall", namely, sex.

The singer, actor and preacher may find self-display among their motives, but let them *direct* their activities to serving the public. The end-motive, not the original drive, cleanses the activity. The politician wants to serve his country, the barrister to serve his client, the social worker to uplift the poor, the missionary to convert the heathen, but, in all cases, honest self-scrutiny would reveal also self-aggrandizement, the desire to boost the ego and to have power or superiority over others.

In the parable of the talents Christ praised ambition, but His teaching made it clear that it is better to let it give one the impetus to help other people and spread the Kingdom of God than to allow it merely to satisfy one's selfishness, sexual hungers, or desire to be praised by the crowd.

It is hypocrisy to bluff oneself about motive, pretending, for instance, that one bought a sexy novel because one wanted to study the literary style of the author!

Integration, mental harmony and inward peace are found by the man who honestly recognizes the many motives which empower his conduct, including those which are purely instinctive, which, after all, were given him to enjoy, but who tries to canalize their energies into activities which truly give him the fullest realization of his own nature and, at the same time, are of service to the community.

Every Job a Divine Vocation

IN A set-up in which God is largely forgotten, the individual Christian often feels baffled and frustrated. Apart from supporting the Church and those philanthropies which press their claims upon them, he wonders what he can do but pray, and he is tempted to think that he counts for nothing in the immense task of making the Kingdom of God conterminous with the life of the world.

Clearly nothing that the organized Church can do by its services, by religious books, by radio or television will effect the needful change. Only as the individual translates his Christianity into terms of the way he does his daily work, and the loving spirit he shows daily in his contact with others, can Christianity leaven the very heavy lump of modern life.

If this seems too idealistic, three thoughts serve to support those who try to make it true.

1. One is that Christ was a carpenter for eighteen years and a preacher for three, and was just as much the Son of God when He made ploughs as when He preached sermons. Before He preached at all the Voice said, "This is my beloved Son in whom I am well pleased."

Often He must have felt frustrated as we do, but so often the stones of today's frustration are just what we need when we come to build tomorrow's temple of achievement. Christ's peerless parables were the fruit of His life in a simple home where garments were patched, bread made and children cared for.

2. A second thought is a right assessment of what is sacred and what is secular. This is determined, not by the job, but by the spirit in which, and the person for whom, the job is done. When I thanked a nurse, in a hospital where I was a patient, for the excellent way she made my bed, she startled me with a very profound sentence. "I don't make it for you," she said, "I make it for our Lord."

When the cobbler mends my shoes honestly, he helps

God to answer my prayer for health in wet weather, and there is no job—unless it is really evil—which cannot become a sacred job, as sacred as that of any priest. Indeed, we can worship God alone, but we can only serve God as we serve our brothers in the everyday life of the world. We do the same work as the non-Christian, but with a richer motive and for a different Master.

3. Beads scattered on a bedroom floor seem to have little significance. Threaded on a necklace there is a unity in which the smallest has its place and importance. Purposelessness in life is mentally crushing, but to believe that wherever we are, God is counting on us to stand for the things of His Kingdom, and that all we do and all that happens to us can, by a right attitude, be threaded on to the string of His purposefulness, is to find a new integration and a mental peace.

Trivial and monotonous events then carry a meaning, and the most insignificant task is precious in His sight, for the thread of a divine purposefulness runs through every part of life.

You Can't Break the Law

WE HAVE come to use a strange phrase. We speak of "breaking the law". Those whose conduct runs counter to the law of the land are said to be lawbreakers. I wonder if in prison they do not meditate on the fact that the law is not broken. Often they are.

We see the point more clearly when we are told that so-and-so is ill because he overworked and "broke the laws of health". Surely it is he who is broken. You cannot break the law. You can break yourself on it.

Chesterton once remarked that if you walk to the edge of the cliffs and keep straight on, you will not break the law of gravity, you will prove it. None of Nature's laws can be *broken*. Each can be either opposed or co-operated with.

Let us not forget that law runs through every part of the universe. This, the religious man argues, is the decree of God. The materialist says it is the nature of things. The fact remains. If it were not so, nothing could be learnt, or relied on when learnt. The universe would be a multiverse and a madhouse. Miracle is never a breaking of law. It reveals the existence and operation of laws not yet recognized, and also the power of one law to influence, deflect and alter the effect of another.

As LAW runs through the physical, psychical and psychological parts of the universe, it runs through the spiritual and moral also. We shall pray better when we understand the laws that govern prayer. Such understanding will silence many silly prayers and increase our faith in others, in the field of healing for instance.

That law governs the moral part of the universe it is very important in these days to recognize. One great indictment of what is miscalled the "new morality"—miscalled since it is neither "new" nor "morality"—is that it does not bring final happiness. The goods promised are never delivered. The road looks attractive but it leads to a "no thoroughfare" notice or sometimes to a precipice.

Behaviour opposed to God's law cannot result in integration of character and joy in living. Promiscuity, fornication and adultery are forms of selfishness, and thus opposed to

63

moral law. They never bring peace of mind. Even forgiveness—a glorious fact offered by God to all men—does not abrogate law. It restores relationship but it does not cancel consequence, though it does change consequence from penal retribution into accepted discipline.

On all levels of man's life, physical, mental and spiritual, healthy contentment is most likely to be found by those who learn God's laws and live in harmony with them.

Mental Poison

It is alleged that the criminals involved in the "Moors Case"[1] had mentally absorbed the writings of the Marquis de Sade and others. Most of us have *tendencies* toward sexual perversion and cruelty and if our reading feeds these tendencies, and subsequently some unexpected situation offers opportunity, it is possible that tendencies could become deeds followed by lifelong regret.

"However could such a man have come to do such a thing?" was asked when a famous person unleashed such tendencies in detected action. The answer was the literature found in his desk after he had fled the country.

Many feel that any kind of censorship is narrow-minded and an attack on liberty. Yet we do not allow people to purchase poisons or dangerous drugs without attempting to prevent them. Why should we not merely allow but

[1] On April 19th 1966, Ian Brady and Myra Hindley were charged with ill-treating three young people, one of them a little girl of ten who—it is alleged—was made to strip naked, and then murdering them. Their bodies were secretly buried on Saddleworth Moor in Yorkshire.

advertise mental poisons—like De Sade's writings for instance—and allow floods of pornography to pollute our bookstalls and subsequently the minds of our fellows?

"What harm can it do? People must learn to know the facts of life." This is said by those who forget that a dead rat in a stinking sewer is a fact, but this is no reason for putting it on the menu.

I think that the happily-married and the sexually-satisfied have no idea of the mental torture of others who are stimulated by mental poisons and yet have no honourable way of finding satisfaction.

He is no friend of society who, by such mental poisons and stimulants, makes life harder for others.

"Hold off from sensuality," says Cicero, "for if you give yourself to it you will be unable to think of anything else." "Fill your thoughts with what is pure and lovable and gracious," says St. Paul. Let us cut out mental poison. What is beautiful and admirable is mental food.

The Caring Church

FAR more people are in distress of mind and body because they are starved of love than because their religious beliefs are in a muddle, or because these have largely been given up. I feel sad when I pass some of the Free Churches and realize that their main doors are open only for a few hours on Sundays, and that if one penetrated through the back or side doors to various meetings one would only be offered devotional succour: prayer, hymns and exhortation.

People must sometimes pass those doors on the way to

commit suicide or on their way to ask their doctor questions which he is not trained to answer. Suicide, so-called nervous breakdown and insanity increase, and below that level of despair, thousands feel frustrated and unhappy because life has become meaningless. More people are ill because they are unhappy than are unhappy because they are ill.

In a sense, the various healing movements, the existence of the Marriage Guidance Councils, the Freemasons and even the Rotary Clubs are a rebuke to the Churches in that men have not found in them an answer to their questions, the satisfaction of their need of fellowship, or adequate scope for their service to others.

THOUGH all these movements have value, the need for them would not have arisen if the Churches had cared more for men and less for creed and ceremony.

Some Churches are splendidly awake to this. The Methodist Church in Highgate, London, has been made a counselling centre. The minister has, helping him, the neighbouring vicar, psychiatrists, lawyers, trained marriage guidance counsellors, medical men and women, all of whom give some time each week, so that it seems to me—and I have watched the experiment closely—that no one could get into any kind of difficulty but the minister could say, "We have just the person to advise you."

It may be said that other social services meet people's needs, the N.H.S. for instance, but few N.H. doctors have time to sit down and listen to a problem that is a real and frantic worry to someone, but which, in the telling and the advice, may take an hour.

In the matter of marriage, how often the banns are called, the ceremony performed and the couple exhorted to attend church. In how few Churches is there any preliminary teaching on sex, on pre-marital intercourse, on birth-control, on family planning, on frigidity and sexual anxiety, on the way to bring up children.

Yet skilled help on all these points is available, and by following the example given, the Church could use her laymen and laywomen more, and at the same time open her arms to all in trouble whatever their creed, colour or nationality. Is not this what the Church exists to do?

The Communist Menace

THE very word "Communism" makes hackles rise, and when it is sometimes hinted that Communists are prolonging a strike, alarm and dismay fill many minds.

Yet few could really state why Communism is a menace. After all, it is a philosophy of life as well as a political creed adopted by over 200 million people, covering a fifth of the earth's surface, and its slogan, "From each according to his ability, to each according to his need", sounds fine. Indeed, a *form* of Communism was practised by the early Church. (Acts 2: 44) But the Christian can have no truck with modern Communism for several reasons.

1. It leaves out God and makes material well-being man's highest aim. Hence it has no place for worship, has no clue to suffering, offers no remedy for despair, and does not acknowledge "sin", forgiveness, or a life after death. Yet it claims to be a way of life as well as a political programme.

2. The *end* for which Communism strives is the State, and Man is only a means to that end. So long as the *end* is achieved it seems not to matter to the Communist if the

means to that end include murder and torture. Man's private freedoms—free speech, and freedom to express views hostile to the party in power—are denied to man where Communism rules. The pulpit, the Press, the classroom, the lecture hall of the college or university, know nothing, under Communism, of the freedom in which we rejoice.

3. The Christian State recognizes that its strength is based on the family as a unit and the truly Christian or Jewish home is the hope of the nation. Communism seems to care nothing about home-life. I am told that in Russia misery is as widespread as it was under the Tsars. The reigning power is a materialistic, godless police state in which thousands of people have been torn from their loved ones and sent to slave labour hundreds of miles from home.

To submit to Communism, then, would be to betray the dead who died for the essential freedoms of mankind. So to submit would also be to betray and deny Christ, who died to make the whole world, without distinction of colour, caste or creed, one great family united by the love of God.

SIGHT AND INSIGHT

Loving God with Our Minds

JESUS CHRIST said that the greatest commandment was that men should love the Lord their God with all their minds. Surely this means that we are never to close our minds against new truth from whatever source it may come, and never to be more eager to preserve the old and traditional than to welcome the new, once the new has authenticated itself to us in an hour of honest examination.

Beauty has a way of authenticating itself. To watch a glorious sunset among the high Alps is to need no arguments before the mind admits beauty. Argument is unnecessary, irrelevant, even offensive. With truth it is different. At the same time a moment comes when argument and insight together have done their work, and about some mighty assertion we whisper within ourselves, "This is true."

I CAN remember when, as a young officer in Mesopotamia in the first world war, after months in the desert away from my fellows, I returned to camp and attended a service in a Y.M.C.A. tent at Basrah. I cannot remember the preacher, but after the service the forgiveness of God became real to me. I *assented* no longer. I *believed*. The assertion that God is loving and forgiving became true for me. Nothing now could take that certainty from me.

This inner certainty is to me the real *authority* in religion.

In the sphere of religion we cannot believe because we are told to do so. We can *assent* through fear, or a desire to please, or because we are too lazy or indifferent to examine. But we can *believe* a statement only when we see it to be true. Religious truth has no authority in personality until it is seen to be true.

THUS we must honour the intellectual integrity of our modern young people, from whom belief is demanded because the Church makes dogmatic assertions. Few tasks are more pressing than that we should restate the fundamental truths of Christianity in such a way as to win the acceptance of the modern, honest mind. Only so can the power, resident in such honest believing, be released into men's lives, giving them the beauty, meaning and purpose which God wills for us all.

Perfect Health

PERFECT health means perfect adjustment to environment. The health of the body is its harmonious adjustment to, and correspondence with, the physical world in which it functions. The health of the eye, for instance, is its harmonious relationship with its relevant environment, which is light. If that harmonious relationship is disturbed, we cannot see, and we truly say, granted that light remains, that the eye is in a state of *dis-ease*. To have healthy lungs means that the lungs are in harmonious relationship with their relevant environment which is air. To have a healthy mind, it must be in a harmonious relationship with its relevant environment, which is truth. If my mind is out of harmony with truth, it is in a state of *dis-ease*.

BUT man is not just body and mind. Part of his non-material personality differentiates him significantly from the animals. It is his soul, the part of his mind which is capable of communion with God, and the health of his soul is its harmonious relationship with its relevant environment which is God.

Perfect health would be perfect relationship with environment at every point of man's being, and since man is a unity of body, mind and spirit (or soul), he cannot reach perfect health if any one relationship is broken or faulty. A man may get along in life with quite a lot of ill-health. A blind or deaf man may do so and even, in his heart, know little of what he is missing. Many people who are mentally ill appear to be quite content.

SIMILARLY, thousands of people appear "to get along" without God or any conscious relationship with Him. But they miss a lot, just as a blind man misses the sunset and the deaf man beautiful music.

If at death, as I believe, one finishes with one's material body, and passes into a life in which mind and soul find fuller functioning, then never to have exercised the soul may be like living in a picture gallery and being unable to see, or attending a concert in which others find unspeakable delight in music, and being unable to hear.

Our remorse then surely justifies Christ's solemn words about outer darkness and weeping and gnashing of teeth. To feel out of it when others are blissfully happy is hell. I think if I knew I was going to attend an age-long concert, I would start learning music.

The Divine Restraint

I HAVE always been deeply impressed by men and women who have immense power and yet who practise a loving restraint. Where God is concerned we should recognize that, again and again, where we wish He would, as it were, burst out of Heaven and claim His rights or achieve His purpose, Love puts a restraint on its own desire.

This is clearly revealed in the repeated restraint of Jesus. The disciples are ready to call down fire from heaven when their Master is not treated courteously. But He restrains them. The devil suggests in the famous temptations that Christ could buy men's allegiance with bread, or magic, or political leadership, but, though He longed for that allegiance, He restrained all impulses which would have bought it. He Himself knew that twelve legions of angels were ready to burst through from the unseen and rescue Him from Pilate and Herod. But no burglars from heaven were allowed to break into the private sanity, even of evil-doers. Christ could have been rescued, but Pilate would have been mad and Herod a gibbering idiot.

Right through the Gospels we are offered the picture of an immensely powerful Being. He can cure the sick, even the leper, at a touch. He can, we are told, raise the dead. But the final picture of Him in the last book of the Bible is of one who is knocking at the door of the proud human heart and yet who will never burgle the sanctuary of the soul and steal its fealty.

This restraint of Jesus reveals the restraint of God. How

immense and terrifying must be His power! The physical universe proclaims it. Atomic energy is but a whisper of God's power in things material. The slow progress we make in the field of psychical research may well be our inability yet to cope with the mighty energies hidden there. Human discovery is only our label for divine revelation and nothing is revealed until we are in sight of power to cope with it. Spiritually we talk of angels and archangels, but it is a good thing we cannot see them. We could not bear apprehension of the purely spiritual yet. But we need not fear. Divine restraint guards us. The brain is probably very like a filter to guard us from knowledge we could not bear, and the five senses shut out a part of the universe which would drive us mad.

WHAT power then God could exert on man! He only had to make religion an instinct and man would crave Him as the hungry crave for bread. He only had to make every divergence from His will incur some dread disease of body or mind to have man subservient at His feet. But God will not burgle the soul, break down our defences, smash our wills or disable our minds. He is content to knock and wait. Indeed, He made the door on which He knocks and *He* fixed the bolt on the inside. When of our own free-will and choice we open every part of our being to Him we make a discovery which all along He wanted us to make: that harmony with Him, loving and being loved, is fullness of life.

The Beckoning Finger

In one of his books, Brunner, the famous theologian, tells us of a vision he had of the progress of humanity. He saw the forward march of the great human family, led by its prophets, saints and seers. But all those who moved forward had their gaze fixed on One far ahead and above them, but facing them and beckoning to them.

Christ is not merely one who two thousand years ago passed across the stage of history, doing lovely deeds, saying inspiring words and living a blameless life, who then disappeared into the unseen, and who inspires us now only by the records of the past. He is not merely the One who having conquered death is with His followers, standing by them and helping them in the problems of their daily life.

He is the Christ of the future. He stands at the end of the road which every man travels. In Him all the trends of true progress find their culmination. He is not only "up to date", to use a common phrase, but "up to" a date we have not yet reached. He will be utterly relevant to life at a point in time which we who are living now will never see on earth. He does not influence us from the past only, or pledge His word to stand by us in the present. He beckons us from what we call the future, and any pathways which do not lead to Him will turn out to be false trails which, if pursued far enough, will bring us to disaster.

All of us who try to follow Him would be wise, whatever our label, to follow His beckoning finger. We may well go back to the records, within and without the New Testament, to make sure of His historic reality. (The evidence for this proves that His historicity is as well grounded as that of Plato.) We are wise to ponder the Resurrection to assure ourselves that He is still alive. But the angel of reality calls to us also, "He goeth before you." Would we not be wise to overhaul Church services, Church organizations, creedal assertions, and, most importantly, our own Christian experience, in case we are hanging about an empty tomb when a living Master has gone on and beckons us to follow Him?

How easy it is to acquiesce in the familiar Church service long after it has anything of the life of the risen Christ in it! How easy to recite ancient affirmations when the living truth has long since left them! Froude, the historian, asks what the health of England would be like if there had been thirty-nine articles of medicine imposed three hundred years ago by Parliament, and if every doctor had been compelled "to compound his drugs by the prescriptions of Henry VIII's physician, Dr. Butts". Instead of moving forward in our apprehension of truth, we try rather pathetically to maintain its historic continuity of expression. We still seek the living truth among its dead forms, and so often the search is fruitless. "Why seek ye the living among the dead?"

Distorted Image

It is not surprising that many people do not really trust God, because the kind of God they picture in their minds is not to be trusted. It is not surprising that people find it hard to love God, for who could possibly love or trust a God who snatches a young mother away from her family by sending her cancer, or who punishes a man with polio for not saying his prayers?

Yet some folk still piously say, "Thy will be done," when these calamities befall, though they spring from the mass ignorance, folly and sin of the whole human family, and are no more personally directed than is a tumble on the football field.

One of the most needful purges for the recovery of true religion is a cleansing of our ideas of God by realizing that no idea about God can possibly be true, even if it is in the Bible, if it is completely out of harmony with the spirit of Christ as the total picture of the New Testament reveals Him. When we see Him in any significant situation we know for certain what the reaction of God is like.

CHRIST was no sentimental, easy-going, complacent Santa Claus, only desirous that everyone should be "happy". His love had steel in it as well as compassion, as the Pharisees found. No one has ever spoken such kind words about sinners or said such terrible things about sin.

But we simply must part for ever with the false picture of God which we have built up from the Old Testament, from false interpretations of the New, and from over-strict parents, schoolteachers, and even childish ideas of eastern despots and tyrants with all-seeing eyes and a sadistic will to punish.

A lady of fifty, who consulted me recently, no sooner mentioned her mother than she related that her mother always put a strap on the table at each mealtime and used it to punish her children for the slightest misdemeanour. Children inevitably make their mental picture of God from

78

the character, teaching and attitudes of those adults who dominate their childhood.

Who can trust and love a God who is always waiting to punish us for our misdoings? One of the factors which prevents the Church becoming the healing fellowship it ought to be is that thousands regard the Church as a respectable society of people who worship a tyrant, who demand belief in the incredible, and who disapprove of all those who fall below a conventional standard of moral behaviour.

Christ loved, understood and accepted all men who sought to follow Him, irrespective of creed, race or moral attainment. The Church must follow Him. It has so misrepresented Him that thousands outside it are better than the God it portrays.

What Is God Like?

In the autobiography of Charles Darwin there is a very sad but significant passage in which he tells us that "very unwillingly" he gave up his belief in Christianity, and then he adds, "I can hardly see how anyone ought to wish Christianity to be true; for, if so, the plain language of the text seems to show that the men who do not believe—and this would include my father, brother, and almost all my best friends—will be everlastingly punished. And this is a damnable doctrine."

I agree with the last sentence, and I am increasingly troubled concerning the number of kindly, splendid, unselfish and thoughtful people who shrink away from the organized Church because they cannot subscribe to the many improbable dogmatic assertions, agreement with which is in some places considered compulsory in anyone calling himself a Christian.

Clearly no one can worship a God whom in his heart he despises as worse than himself. And any God who punished everlastingly someone because he could not "believe", or, indeed, for any other reason, would be a despicable tyrant. No serious-minded student of the Gospels can legitimately soften down Christ's estimate of the dark seriousness of sin. But two clues for finding out what God was like were given by Christ. One was to watch Him in any significant situation, for He said, "He that hath seen Me hath seen the Father". (John 14: 9) This does not mean snatching at isolated sentences doubtfully ascribed to Him, and often, I am convinced, unrecognizably distorted by the prejudices and complexes of the writers. It means allowing the *total impact* of the four Gospels on our minds to produce a self-consistent image of Him from which we can deduce the nature of God.

THE other clue Jesus gave us was that of our own natures. "If you then, bad as you are, know how to give your children what is good for them, *how much more* generous will your Heavenly Father be." (cf. Luke 11: 13, N.E.B.) This passage, together with the parables, ought to have banished some of the heresies about hell, the view that cancer is "the will of God", that suffering is God's punishment for sin, and so on. Who can trust, love or worship a God who does things for which a man would be locked up in gaol or sent to a criminal lunatic asylum?

Following these clues we shall have to put many isolated texts into a mental box labelled, "Awaiting Further Light", but at any rate we shall not be worshipping a non-existent bogy who stoops to methods of getting His own way which we rightly regard as despicable.

If we keep on looking at Jesus and into our own hearts we shall know what God is like. Let us dare to believe the best about God. We cannot think better than the truth.

God's Secret Ally

WHEN, on lovely summer days, I see the curling frond of fern or bracken lifted toward the sky, it seems like a finger beckoning to the sun as if to say, "Help me! I can only be my true self as I respond to you." So, the power of a mighty celestial body, ninety million miles away, wins a response from a humble, earthborn plant. Life and growth develop. Beauty is born.

It seems to me a parable of our relationship with God. Deep in every human heart He has a mysterious and secret ally. It is man's power to respond to Him. Let me list five ways in which this happens.

1. *In our quest for truth* we reach from time to time a point at which truth is *possessed* by our whole being. It is a spiritual experience rather than the end of an argument. Something we have long known with the intellect becomes what Shelley called "a truth of the emotions" as well. God's secret ally whispers, in regard to some great truth such as forgiveness, "This is true", and the difference is as immense as the change in the heart of John Wesley when, having preached forgiveness for years, he could write in his diary, as if it were a new experience, "I *knew* God for Christ's sake had forgiven me."

2. *In our recognition of beauty*. What strange ally of God is this within the soul which moves us sometimes almost to tears at some breathtaking scene in nature, or a child's face, or a violin's lament, or a woman's voice?

3. *In our admiration of goodness*. Whatever level of character we ourselves may or may not have achieved, everyone admires the unselfish act, the brave deed, the self-forgetting sacrifice. However muddled our thinking may be on a hundred matters, and however we may differ from one another on a hundred topics, no one could ever convince us that our sense of values was wrong and that beastliness and selfishness were *better* than love. God has a secret ally in every heart which we could call the approval of goodness.

4. *In our response to conscience*. When all has been taken into account concerning the lowly, utilitarian origins of conscience; when all has been said of terrible deeds done by men of distorted conscience; we know in our hearts that we did this or that because we wanted to do it though we knew it was wrong. That awareness is God's secret ally, ever pleading His cause.

5. *In our surrender to God*. When, in some secret act of surrender, we say "yes" to God and open every room in the house of life to His sway, we acknowledge that God's secret ally has won. Then a strange peace floods into our hearts. We feel like a man who after much wandering has come home where he belongs and where he is accepted, loved and understood.

I have taken many words to say what St. Paul said in one sentence: "The Spirit Himself beareth witness with our spirits that we are children of God." We *belong*.

Are You an Atheist?

I AM not writing here about the agnostic. I have a great respect for him and go a long way with him, for he says, about God and religion, "I do not know." Some agnostics would say, "Man *cannot* know." Such an attitude seems to me a healthy corrective to the attitude of insect man, strutting on an insignificant speck of matter in a universe whose vastness makes the brain reel, who claims presumptuously that he can put a tape of creedal words around the nature and activities of its Creator.

But even that presumption is less than that of the atheist who, possessing much arrogance but no logic, declares, "There is no God." Clearly no one can prove such a negative.

A man has a strange mentality who can look up to the night sky or down on the emerging daffodils; who can listen to the haunting melody of a master-musician, or study the migration of birds; who can look into the face of his first-born babe, or mark the strange peace that so often fills the eyes of the dying, and yet say with complete assurance, "There is no God."

Having talked, through the years, with many self-styled atheists, I have come to the conclusion that the true species does not exist. "Atheism" turns out to be an emotional reaction in the same category as neurotic illness and with the same kind of causation. So, years ago, a woman rushed into my vestry and declared that there was no God, but her "atheism" had only developed after her husband had been turned out of the choir!

Dr. Bernard Hart, in *The Psychology of Insanity*, tells of the "atheism" of a Sunday school teacher which developed only when a fellow-teacher became engaged to a girl whom the "atheist" had marked down for his own conquest!

WE WHO believe in God have been scorned for "wishful thinking". "You wish there were such a Being, to love you, guide you, care for you and vindicate at last your sense of values," we are told, "so you invent one. But no such Being exists outside your own imagination."

I often think of the laddie, a "displaced person", who spent years in a refugee camp and dreamed nightly of a father whom he was told was dead and did not exist. It was a lie, and at last the broken family was united. When the boy found his father, the reality was better than the dream.

Men long for God. Does longing prove them wrong? If fundamental deception be ruled out, my hunger for bread points to the likelihood that bread exists. What of man's hunger for God? It proves nothing, but it is very significant, and I wonder if man is capable of even imagining anything that is really better than the truth. "I will not believe," said Sir Oliver Lodge, "that it is given to man to have thoughts higher and nobler than the real truth of things."

The Creed of a Christian Agnostic

NO ONE will deny that the religious thought of today is terribly confused. What with *Honest to God*, *Soundings*, *Objections to Christian Belief*, and certain sermons from Southwark, it is no wonder that the layman wonders just where he is. Further, even moral standards seem to be altering, which makes the confusion worse confounded.

At such a time of widespread doubt, I find it helpful to set down some of the things of which I feel quite certain, even though I am painfully aware of the charge of over-simplification.

1. I believe that God exists. My mind cannot accept the thought that the universe is an unpurposed accident, and that man's sense of values has no source outside the chemistry of his brain.

2. I believe that there is Mind behind the universe. Though I can understand little about that Mind, it must be greater than I. Such a Mind must be "He" rather than "it", and must be "Love" rather than hate or indifference or cruelty or incompetence.

3. I believe in the divinity of Christ because if I load all the evidence about Him on board the word "human", the ship sinks. It cannot carry so heavy a cargo of meaning. I admit I do not know what "divine" means, save to say that Christ is the Man in history who to a far greater extent than, and in quite a different way from, others, fills the word "God" with meaning. I am convinced that Christ is the world's Saviour, in the sense that He committed Himself to win humanity into harmony with God and is still at work to that end. His death was both a revelation of the sacrificial nature of love and a pledge that He will go to love's utter-most to win us to unity with God.

4. I believe that sin is a grisly fact in the world, which cannot be dismissed by flattering psychological labels. I suggest that anything is "sin" if its wide adoption would wreck an ideal society, and if we should feel ashamed of it in the presence of Christ.

5. I believe that God's forgiveness is one of the most

blessed and therapeutic experiences in the world and that it is offered to all who seek it whatever they have done, or whatever they believe.

6. I believe that our relationship with God, which the very word "religion" connotes, is the most important thing in the world, and that we can put it right today and start a new, rich, meaningful life now.

7. I believe that each individual is precious to God, and that a divine undefeatable purpose is being worked out in every life: a life that goes on after death. A thousand things happen to us which are not "the will of God", but nothing can happen to us which can defeat His purposes at last.

All this gives me as much as I need and seems to me the essential credo of Christianity. About the rest I am content to be agnostic.

A Chain of Evidence

I HAD many letters about my article on atheism, and find myself very attracted to those whose denial is one of a bogy who certainly does not exist, but whom they had heard called "god". Such "atheists" help us to find the truth about the real God, and to exclude false ideas about Him. Many letters challenge me to prove that God exists. I wish I could, but no "proof", in the ordinary meaning of the word, exists. For me, the only "proof" is that certain experiences of my own, and even more convincingly, of others, do not make sense if I deny His existence.

Yet, even in this limited space, I would like to offer a chain of evidence, and, if it is hopelessly unsound at any point, I should sincerely like to be told where and why.

1. To me the universe bears some marks of a purposeful mind. Much appears chaotic and meaningless, but one tidy bed in a dormitory of unmade beds suggests purposeful activity at work. I do find *some* phenomena which evidence order rather than accident, and purpose anywhere must mean purpose everywhere. Such order seems improbable without design.

2. Inasmuch as I can detect, even if rarely, purposefulness in the universe, the mind behind it must, in some ways, work like my own, or I should not detect order and purpose to be such.

3. This mind must possess at least the qualities in my mind, which, if I know anything, I know to be "good". I *know* that love is better than hate, or cruelty, or selfishness, or indifference. If this mind is not loving I am *better* than it is.

4. Similarly, though it may be inadequate to call this mind "personal", if I call it a "cosmic force", or "the absolute", or an "ultimate reality", or even "the ground of all being", my words take me further from the truth than does the word "he", for this mind must be "he" rather than "it"; must be more than I mean by "personal", but certainly not less.

5. If this loving mind is purposeful anywhere in the universe, surely this is likely to be manifested in human lives. Even I have a purpose in the lives of those who owe their being to me and call me "father".

6. If a child, who has just learned to play *The Joyful Peasant* with one hand, criticized Beethoven, and a boy who continually failed G.C.E. in arithmetic said that Einstein was no mathematician, I should question their right to deny. On the lowest level of assessment, Jesus Christ was the world's

greatest spiritual genius. If I, at my insignificant level of intellectual ability, spiritual insight and moral attainment, imaginatively said to Him: "When, on the Cross, you said, 'Father, into Thy hands I commit my spirit', there was really no one there. You only *wished* you had a Father. I know better. There is no God." Well, I think I should deserve the word "arrogant". I should feel more presumptuous than if I had told Beethoven he could not write music, or Einstein that he had got his sums wrong!

Sight and Insight

Luke, the doctor, tells a moving story of a blind beggar who would not be silenced. (18: 35 ff.) When at last he got to Jesus he naturally had only one request: "Lord, that I may receive my sight." His request was granted. What with his own faith, the touch of Christ and the expectancy of the crowd, the blindness—the nature of which we are not told—was banished. One can only imagine his joy at seeing again the faces of friends, the blue sky, the green trees, even the dusty Jericho road, and, surely not least, the face of Christ.

Such a story always makes one prize, with gratitude to God, the privilege of physical sight. How poor our summer holidays would be if we could not gaze on mighty mountains that somehow satisfy the soul; if dawn and sunset, moonlight on the sea, or the silent majesty of the stars could not penetrate our shrouded life; if the faces of loved ones, or the flowers, the birds, the streams and trees and meadows could carry no message and bring no healing to the town-sick spirit. Above all, for myself, I feel most grateful that I can *read*. Endlessly, ideas which are the food of the mind and soul are at one's disposal in books.

YET, we all need to pray the prayer, "Lord, that I may receive my sight." Recently, as a group of young people discussed moral problems with me, a boy, leaving school that summer, commented on a prostitute who had been much in the news, "I think we ought to remember that she was once a pure and lovely young girl who probably cherished high ideals." I silently prayed, "Lord, that I may receive my sight." I had never thought of her thus. But of course the boy was right. Behind that proud churchman's egotism, behind that selfish materialist's quest for wealth, behind that teenager's moral uncertainty and that gossip's waspish tongue is a soul loved by God and capable of nobility and saintliness.

"Lord, that I may receive my sight!" Then I shall see more quickly my brother's need and his possibilities. I shall see the admirable qualities in the folk who don't attract me. I shall see the shop-girl and the manager, the bus conductor and the director, the policeman and the magistrate, the waitress and the duchess, the dustman and the doctor, as *persons* dear to God, as souls of immortal worth. I shall see the foreigner as my neighbour and the enemy as God's child.

I need not only sight but insight. Then I shall see God's way with the nations, and, slowly, discern a pattern in my own bewildering life. I shall see that God is still in charge of His world and that no power of evil can snatch away His final victory or furnish grounds for human despair. *Appearance* need blind me no longer, for still God answers the trusting cry, "Lord, that I may receive my sight."

Messengers of the Invisible

I READ a sentence one day which seemed worth pondering: "The obscure, dark and painful turns given to our lives are also messengers of the Invisible, but we sometimes have to wait for Eternity before the mystery is solved" (Erich Schick).

No wise man can make out a case that everything that happens to him is the will of God in the sense of being God's intention. Misused free-will leads to false choices and subsequent trouble. Folly leads to disaster. Sin leads to unhappiness. Our interdependence means that when one man discovers penicillin we all reap unmerited benefit. Similarly, if one woman uses thalidomide, an innocent baby suffers unmerited handicap. As you sit and read these words, pause to remember that tens of thousands of people, through no fault of their own, are hungry and ill, lonely and frustrated, handicapped and impoverished, while what God wills is perfect health of body, mind and spirit for all His children; the perfect functioning of all their powers and the complete fulfilment of all their possibilities. God is the supreme Artist, and no artist *wills* imperfection in that which he creates.

Maybe, as Schick says, we shall "have to wait for Eternity before the mystery is solved". Immense faith is demanded and it must not be a faith which collapses when things go wrong. As Dr. John Oman wrote: "Until faith in Providence as mere beneficence breaks down, the faith which reconciles us to God in the face of every conceivable evil cannot arise. But then, nothing whatsoever in the world is omitted from what works together for good."

MY OWN thought of God is of One who has no favourites—not even the saints—who is at work in every detail of His universe, which is yet far from being what He wants it to be. He will not make man incapable of folly, or ignorance, or sin, for then man would be less than God's plan for him. God will allow accident and natural disaster, but my faith is that God will not allow anything to happen which cannot be finally woven into a plan, grand beyond our present conceiving. Further, I believe that every significant happening in life carries a message from the unseen. God is like a Signalman who, to flash a message, uses lamps which He Himself neither made nor lit.

"My Father," said Jesus, "has never yet ceased His work." (John 5: 17 N.E.B.) In the light of this I have to be patient while a plan slowly moves to a promised perfection, ultimately to be achieved in eternity, remembering that Omnipotence does not mean that everything that happens is God's will, but that nothing that can happen is incapable of being woven into His plan. And, when dark experiences befall me from which I cannot honourably escape, my wisest question surely is: "What is God trying to say to me in all this, and how can I react to it so as to further His cause and maintain my own inward peace?"

All life's happenings can be "messengers of the Invisible".

Believing, Behaving and Loving

EVERY denomination naturally seeks to promote its own beliefs and method of worship. Otherwise there would be little point in its separateness. Yet when one remembers that in the ritual of Rome, and in the silence of the Quakers, in the freedom of the Free Churches and in the imposed order of the Anglicans, men find reality, one is bound to conclude that the mode of worship cannot be important. When one remembers that Christ holds the loyalty of men whose views are irreconcilable, like Pope John and General Booth, Albert Schweitzer and Billy Graham, John Knox and Fr. Ronald Knox, one is bound to conclude that theological opinion is not of primary importance either.

I can and do believe *in* my friends without sharing their opinions, and I can and do believe *in* the Lord Jesus Christ without glibly assenting to statements made about Him, many of which He never made about Himself. They have been attached to Him by the Church, in some cases after centuries.

It is pleasant, in an article on the Christian religion, to quote the Buddha who said, "Believe nothing because a so-called wise man said it. Believe nothing because a belief is generally held. Believe nothing because it is written in ancient books. Believe nothing because it is said to be of divine origin. Believe only what you yourself judge to be true." Indeed, the only authority there is in religion is that of perceived truth. We only really *believe* when truth authenticates itself in the mind, though assent often passes for belief. Hence Jesus never demanded the acceptance of theological propositions, but offered a transforming friendship within which the essential truths of Christianity were born, and grew up in the minds of His men, as we must allow truth to possess us.

SIMILARLY, in regard to bad behaviour, Christ was slow to condemn because He separated the person from the behaviour. When we review our own misdeeds we never identify ourselves with our bad behaviour. "I'm not *really* like that," we say. If we wholly identify people with their bad behaviour we shall condemn *them* instead of what they do, and so make a chasm where what is needed is a bridge over which love can pass to heal and to redeem.

We are often bound to disapprove of what people do, but if they feel that we reject *them* they will react, either by withdrawal or by angry and violent behaviour. How terribly the Church has sinned by disapproving of people because they do not believe or behave as we think they should!

The Church, primarily, should be the loving community opening its fellowship and offering loving acceptance to men and women, whatever they believe and whatever they do. And by loving I don't mean anything patronizing or sentimental. I mean an unbreakable goodwill that restores for men belief in themselves. This Christ *did* assert as fundamental. "By this shall all men know that ye are my disciples, if ye have love one to another."

God No Copyright of Religion

ONE of the most unfortunate impressions the churches have made by attitude and organization is to let men suppose that there is an area of activity fenced off from the miscalled "secular world" and called "religious work".

If a man holds office in any branch of the church, if he attends its services, prays, reads his Bible, teaches in the Sunday school or conducts a Bible class, then religious authority praises him. He is called religious. He is said to give a portion of his time to God, although the rest of his work is in "the world".

A truly religious outlook would enable us to see that the whole world is God's and that all our time is His. There is nothing secular but evil, and the man who meets the challenges of every day in the spirit of Christ is truly Christian, even though church services bore and nauseate him, its creeds offend his intellectual integrity, and its hymns make him feel ill.

A doctor visiting his patients, a teacher teaching, a mother caring for her children and her home, and men doing what is called the secular work of the world can all be engaged in what is far more accurately named "divine service" than that which is so designated on the church notice board as being held at 11 and 6.30 on Sundays. We can worship God by ourselves but we can only *serve* Him in service to men.

Jesus was as truly living the life of a Son of God when He made yokes and ploughs, as when He made and preached sermons. On some days His supreme service to the Kingdom of God was to make a door that would close quietly, and a yoke that did not chafe the shoulders of the beast which bore it. My Christian shoemaker helps God answer the prayers of His people for health in wet weather, and in my view he is as truly a minister of God as the man who hands me the Holy Communion.

I AM sure some devout souls think that heaven will be like an endless service in church. God forbid! He is not the copyright of religion. Mathematicians should feel that the glory of God is revealed in their calculations. Musicians should tell themselves that Beethoven's Ninth Symphony is far more eloquent of God than some pages of the Bible. Sculpture and painting, poetry and song, fellowship and fun, work conscientiously done, these too are sacred things and, because they are the hem of His garment, healing and joy can flow through them from Him.

Let us stop thinking of religion as something which a small minority of people happen to like doing on Sundays, and strive to show that religion is conterminous with the whole of life. Such religion would change the world, integrate man's personality and make sense of his life.

Nature's Mockery

How eagerly we all look forward to holidays—some days of escape to mountain, moor and sea! Many secretly hope that resting in the country or on the beach may do more than physical and mental good. They hope that inner conflicts will be resolved, that moral tangles will get sorted out, that sins will be forgiven. They cry with Job, "Where shall wisdom be found and where is the place of understanding?—But the deep saith, 'It is not in me,' and the sea saith, 'It is not with me'." And the mountains and the moors say the same.

It is my opinion that Nature's beauty may provide a very helpful setting for the recovery of the soul's health but that the healing comes from a far deeper Source. If Nature's beauty of itself brought holiness, men would be most holy where Nature is most beautiful. This is far from the truth. The crime records of the country-side show that the population is as prone to evil in the country as in the sooty city where none of Nature's loveliness calls to the soul, and I have myself seen orgies of cruelty taking place where flowers gem the forest floor, where mighty trees lift lovely arms to heaven and where the blue sky is pierced by the unstained glory of mountain peaks clothed in eternal snow.

Is IT not rather true that Nature reflects the inner mood of the soul? The sea on a summer day seems to shout back the gleeful laughter of the bathers and to minister to their happiness, but to one troubled in mind the restless waves add restlessness, and to one whose dear one has been drowned the sea is cruel and treacherous. Mountains may be symbols of spiritual strength to many, but in Norway on an autumn evening, their men away fishing, mountains increase, with their terrifying precipices, the anxiety of women waiting at home. The stars to lovers shine in benign approval but to hungry Hiawatha and his friends it was very different,

> "And the hungry stars in Heaven
> Like the eyes of wolves glared at them."

WHEN, as a young minister, I returned from the East to take charge of a down-town church in Manchester, I was filled with youthful indignation in regard to poverty and slums. At last I arranged for a tubercular patient, a young girl, to live in a country cottage. There was a lovely garden and a perfect view of distant hills. But when I went to see her she burst out, "Take me back to Manchester. I hate the country. Look at those unfriendly hills! I've only a few months to live I want *friends* to talk to. I want someone who understands!" I learned a lot from her. I took her back to Manchester. She died among friends. Above all, she found a Friend who perfectly understood.

Three Lies About Time

At certain times of the year many people meditate on Time. Let me try to expose three lies about it.

1. "Time will heal," we say. This is a lie. If the body be wounded, the healing forces of nature will often bring healing *in* time. Even then skilled help is often needed, as everyone knows who shattered his elbow and left the cure to Time! A useless limb has often taught men that Time cannot heal. So, in the mind, Time has never healed a repressed complex or a broken heart, though *in* Time we learn to cope with both. We learn a lot *in* Time, but Time does not make men wise. It only makes a young fool into an old fool; a young sinner into an old one. If Time healed body, mind and spirit, old age for all would spell perfection, but many with Hood and Wordsworth know they are "farther off from Heaven" than when they were children. Time is like a room *in* which things happen, and it has just as little influence upon them.

2. A second lie is that which supposes that Time has lasting reality. A few considerations would reveal a fallacy here. Many dream of what we *call* the past or future. It is present to them. Many fear that a loved one, long since dead, will have become unrecognizable, forgetting that he no longer lives in the room called Time but in another called Eternity.

"They shall grow not old, as we that are left grow
    old,
    Age shall not weary them, nor the years condemn."

Many think that if God knows now, what they are going to

do in the future, that future is inevitable, forgetting that He knows what they did in the past, but His knowing did not determine their doing, and that past, present and future all stand in the same relationship to Him. I *know* that if I hold out a bone to a starving dog he will move towards it. But my knowing does not determine his action. His hunger does. God's knowing does not determine my action. My action, whether past, present or future, determines His knowing.

3. A third lie would have us believe that long years are an advantage. We take over this illusion from the Old Testament, where longevity was the reward of the righteous, and, in the fifth commandment, the reward for honouring one's parents. (Methuselah must have been incredibly kind to the old folks at home!) But who would rather live to be a decrepit old man of ninety, than a Shelley or a Keats who thrilled the world and died in youth?

LET us regard Time as a room in which many things happen, remembering that the way we react to them is more important than they are in themselves, even if we call them disasters. Or let us regard Time as a university in which we are required to qualify for the next phase. Let us never speak of "loss of life". There is no such thing, but only life in another room. And, in a true sense, Life *begins* when Time ends.

God the Weaver

DURING the first world war, as a young officer, my duties took me to Persia and I had the privilege of watching the weaving of the famous Persian carpets. With a medical student who knew the language, I saw a rug set up vertically. Facing the side on which people would tread was the artist. On the reverse side, planks were placed, on which quite young boys sat ready for work. Work went forward, the artist directing the boys who put in the stitches.

I was made to understand that if a worker made a mistake, either in colour or in design, the artist would not necessarily interfere but would weave the mistake into the pattern. The latter might be different, but, my interpreter explained, not necessarily less beautiful, if the artist were a great artist.

When the workers have finished their work on the wrong side of the carpet, where, admittedly, there is little sign of pattern or plan, the artist calls them down from their plank and brings them round to the right side, to see what he has achieved through their labours, including their mistakes.

The experience became a parable for me. Working, as we do, in positions from which we can see little plan or pattern or purpose in human life, the Great Artist nevertheless is weaving all into meaningfulness, and at the end of the day will take us to a point from which we can see all He has done with our sorrows, our frustrations and our pain, whether caused by our own mistakes and sins, or by those of others.

Was ever a plan more terribly ruined for those on the spot than when Jesus of Nazareth was crucified? Was He not God's Son who had come to do God's will and redeem the world, and was not the plan ruined by wickedness? Yet the Great Artist wove even *that* into the centre of a pattern which now we call "the redemption of the world by our Lord Jesus Christ".

So I have to leave my own sorrows, disappointments, sins and failures in the hands of the Weaver whom I cannot see and whose plans seem marred, knowing that an hour will dawn, sooner or later, when I am shown *His* finished work, and realize that nothing can happen to me which robs Him of His glory or me of my adoration of His power. "With them that love Him," said St. Paul, "God co-operates, *in all things* for good". (Romans 8: 28)

The Hour of Knowing

THE publication of a new life of Rupert Brooke must have reminded thousands of my generation of the magic of his poems and of their effect upon us in the first world war. A line in his poem *The Voice* has haunted me for fifty years: "I knew that this was the hour of knowing."

Again and again in our lives there are outstanding periods, whether of an hour or only a moment, when certainty dawns. Thus once, after a week of cloud and rain, I saw Everest at sunrise, and though the clouds returned, the certainty remained. *I knew it was there.*

There comes a moment when we know we must follow this path, marry that girl, choose this job, undertake that training, just as in that magnificent film shown on TV, *Faith on the River Kwai*, a young officer *knew* he must be a parson.

Sometimes it is an hour of faith in the midst of frustration. Life wearily drags on for thousands who feel they can never express the love or the achievement that lies dormant within them. Frustration nearly presses them down into cynicism, apathy or despair. I often think of Jesus, tied to a carpenter's shop for twenty years, when He longed to convey the message that burned ever more brightly in His breast. His hour had not yet come. Then came God's moment. He was free to be all He had it in Him to be, and all the years of monotonous labour would prove an asset in His opportunity.

For us all, I believe, God's moment comes, when, as it were, God puts His hand on our shoulder and says, "Now I want you", and we know, in that hour of knowing, that everything borne, everything suffered and endured, all the frustration and all the pain will prove to have been frozen assets which in our hour of destiny, this side of death or the other, will find their place in a plan we could not discern. Blessed are those who keep on watching and listening, for the hour will come.

Sometimes the hour of knowing is one in which we correct our perspective; when we realize that the things that upset us are trifles and that little things, so called, are of eternal worth.

At my beloved City Temple we prayed one Sunday night for a saintly lady, desperately ill. When her son, a scientist, returned home from church she was no better but she said this: "While you were at church a great peace fell upon me and *I knew that my illness didn't matter any more.*" She had had an "hour of knowing", in which it became clear that dying was no more important than moving house, and indeed very like it.

God grant us hours of knowing! The New English Bible has a pregnant translation of Luke 19: 44, "You did not recognize God's moment when it came."

THE INCENTIVES OF PRAYER

Is Prayer a Waste of Time?

It can seem to be, in church when the mind boggles at the language used, or alone when the mind refuses to do anything but wander. But in both it can be as valuable as air to lungs and rather like it. For science knows nothing of life which persists in an organism if its environment is permanently denied. Without air the lungs die. God is the Environment of the soul. Probably we cannot totally shut Him out, but real prayer can be like a "breath of fresh air" to the stifled soul of man.

For private prayer I love the idea of Florence Allshorn: "To sit quietly before God doing nothing, only fixing the will gently on some expressive phrase like . . . 'Father, here am I and here are You,' makes all the difference." She likens this to lying in the sun and surrendering one's body to it, and she believes one is affected spiritually at the centre of being, just as by sheer, relaxed surrender, the sun changes the colour of the skin. I agree.

For myself, I find that I don't pray for things. This is not humility or superiority. It must be right for a child to tell his Father what he wants. It is just that I feel He knows that already, and that wordless communion, say, during a lonely walk along the shore, gets me further. At the same time I want to make progress in praying, and perhaps we can assess whether we are moving forward if our prayer moves from saying to God, "Give me" to "Make me", and then to "Show me", and finally "Use me".

I THINK God does use us when we pray for others, but all I can do, say, on praying for a sick friend, is to ask God, who uses the skill of doctors and nurses, to use my love and caring to change the deep mind of the patient from despair, darkness, fear and so on, to optimism, light and trust. This may make all the difference between recovery and death. My City Temple congregation used to join in such prayers, sometimes with heart-warming results. One critic called it "telepathy", but that no more rules out God than to speak of "evolution" rules out His creative power. He who discovers wires leading to an electric bell is foolish to deduce that there is no battery! If nurses, by means of an oxygen tent, can assist God's healing power in a case of respiratory disease, why should not positive, loving thought directed to a patient change his deep mind with good result? No one cures except God. The important question to answer is how can we best co-operate with Him in the case of a particular patient?

IT IS important to remember that the essence of prayer is communion. It is no cure-all or certain way of obtaining what we desire. For example, God will not allow us to dispense with medical research by putting a penny-prayer in the slot, as it were, and drawing out a cure. If I get appendicitis I hope they will send for a surgeon rather than a bishop! A friend of mine rightly said that if he were drowning he would rather see on the bank a burglar who could swim than a bishop who couldn't!

Prayer has often been misused because a more demanding

response to a situation was needed. But I don't see how it can be a *complete* waste of time for a child to turn to his Father in any time of need.

Praying for People

PRAYING for people must often puzzle even the devout. It so often seems fruitless. We pray for A and he recovers. We pray for B and he dies, and we don't know why in either case. The cynic says A would have recovered in any case and we know no convincing answer. We pray every Sunday that the Queen may have "health and wealth long to live", but the nation supplies the wealth, and the longevity of the Royal Family is no longer than that of any other. A million people regularly prayed for peace before the last war began.

Two replies occur at once to the Christian. He is commanded by Christ to pray; not necessarily to understand whether it will "work" in the way he wishes; not necessarily to understand at all. Secondly, he knows that Christ Himself prayed for others. The Christian can hardly say, "I am not asked to follow Him there."

All the same, it helps if we can understand only a little of how prayer may "work". A nurse who rigs up an oxygen tent for a patient does not cure him. Indeed, all healing is of God alone. But she does co-operate with God in giving the healing energies of God a better chance. Intercession may be a means whereby we supply the "oxygen" of our love and faith, our courage and optimism, our buoyancy and caring, and let them surround the mind and soul of the person for whom we pray. And this may be just the co-operation which

God asks from us to achieve His own will. Sincere prayer for another cannot be wasted. But, of course, we cannot suppose that it will always overcome evil. Nor, in the field of disease, can we suppose that God will allow it to be a lazy substitute for medical and psychological research.

DURING the Great Plague, thousands prayed ardently that God would heal their dear ones. If He had done so, plague might still be with us. Men would have put—as it were—a prayer in the slot, drawn out a cure and never bothered further to find out those causes which lead to prevention. Maybe cancer stands now where plague stood then.

I know no words which carry more meaning in less verbiage than the pregnant saying of St. Augustine: "Without God, we cannot. Without us, God will not." Wherefore let us co-operate with God in prayer, not overcoming a divine reluctance, but co-operating with a divine willingness.

Telepathy and Prayer

TELEPATHY is the communication of ideas from one mind to another without the use of the senses. In my opinion, the evidence for it is conclusive. It seems to me a fact, though little understood, that in certain circumstances minds which are on the same "wave-length", and especially when they are under the stress of some benign emotion, do at times communicate messages to one another, geographical distance making no difference.

Whately Carrington, who has written much on telepathy, bases his explanation on the undoubted fact that at deep levels, human, and indeed insect, bird and animal minds are connected with one another. As Professor Price of Oxford wrote, "It is nonsense to suppose that minds are spatially separate entities. Minds are not objects in space. On the unconscious level there are no sharp boundaries between one mind and another."

If then the members of a congregation are sincerely praying for a sick child (I say "child" because his mind is more vulnerable to the invasion of external ideas) and praying positively, their minds filled with thoughts of health, hope, buoyancy and courage, the mind of the patient may be so changed in tone as tremendously to strengthen his resistance to disease. Everyone knows nowadays the importance of the mental attitude in disease.

ALL healing is of God, but God has ordained that man shall co-operate with Him. In illness the doctors, nurses and surgeons co-operate on physical levels and the psychiatrist on mental levels. The religious man who loves his sick brother can co-operate with God on mental and spiritual levels.

He is not telling God something He does not know. He is not calling on God to intervene with a miracle. He is not overcoming a divine reluctance. He is co-operating with a divine willingness as the doctor is, but he is doing so on the mental and spiritual levels just as the doctor and nurse are co-operating on the physical level.

No one should deduce from what I have written above that prayer is "only telepathy". This would be to make the same mistake as our grandfathers made when scientists first used the magic word "evolution". They thought evolution banished God from the creative process whereas it only described that process.

Telepathy only describes the mental machinery which God uses in some cases when we make intercession for our friends. For most of us, however,—children of a scientific age—faith is enormously strengthened and prayer encouraged if a measure of understanding is available as to how prayer for another sometimes works.

THE CHRISTIAN YEAR

Herod Still Threatens

WHEN we approach the festival of the Child, let us remember that the welfare of the world tomorrow depends on what is happening to children throughout the world today. Let us realize that evil threatens them. The spirit of Herod is not dead, and the Christ Child calls us not so much to grow sentimental over His cradle and our Christmas tree, but to minister to His little brothers and sisters.

There are still poor children. A friend writes to me of an area in Europe where almost all are poor and where the price of coffee and tea puts them in the list of prohibitive luxuries, and everything else is in proportion. There are areas where people live and die on the pavement, and children are born there without even the warmth of a straw-filled manger.

There are still unwanted children. What can be the mental reaction of black children at being kept separated from whites? I read of a white couple in South Africa who had the effrontery to adopt a black child! It is reported that they were made to leave the country. Yet they acted in the name and spirit of Him for whom "there was no room in the inn".

There are still starving children. In a world so stocked with food that merely to store it costs millions, the food wasted is one-fifth of all that is produced. That waste would feed the whole population of Africa for a whole year. In such a world, four people out of five are hungry, and one person dies of starvation every five seconds. Over a score of people have died of hunger while you have been reading this article. We can get a Telstar into space but we can't get surplus food to starving children. Yet Bethlehem means "the house of bread".

There are children in our midst being mentally and morally poisoned. With the decrease in religious influence, parental example and home discipline, our children are being poisoned by pornography and promiscuity before they reach their middle-teens.

Yet on children depends the coming of the Kingdom of God, or, in other words, the true welfare of the world. From His cradle the Christ Child pleads for them.

Christmas Magic

ON Christmas Eve the magic spreads into almost every home in the land. In the hearts of children it starts days before. Even the hardest-hearted "grown-up" yields a little to its influence. On Christmas Day it reigns. It isn't just a "holiday feeling". August Bank Holiday contains no magic like this.

If dwellers from another planet ever come to earth to find out what we are like, I hope that, if this country is visited, it will be on Christmas Eve or Christmas Day. For when the Christmas magic falls upon us, we are at our best. It is as though our sense of values had suddenly been exalted and changed. Kindness is at a maximum, cruelty all but extinct. Charity, goodwill, tolerance, sympathy, indeed all the lovely virtues, seem to rule our hearts, and selfishness, pride, intolerance, meanness and the spirit of grab fall away.

It is as though a woman should go to a drawer and find in it a string of lovely jewels, lying dusty and disused, and lift them up and wipe the dust from them and wear them round her throat so that all could rejoice in their beauty and recognize their worth. But alas, so often on the day after Boxing Day they go back into the drawer and are forgotten. By the time we have burnt the holly and put the paper-caps on the fire, Scrooge is himself again and our old pagan sense of values is re-established.

No one who can remember his childhood can ever forget how that Christmas magic possessed him. For me it reached its climax when, at a time that seemed the middle of the night, I was awakened by the "waits" playing on brass instruments, "Hark, the herald angels sing!" I was physically thrilling all over with the Christmas magic and dropped off to sleep again as one who has known an experience of the supernatural.

On the next morning what an anticlimax it was when the waits came to collect their money! The man who played the trombone and who, when he played that final, deep, satisfying "G" out there in the darkness, opened for one small listener the very kingdom of heaven, looked anything but supernatural! How soon the magic passes!

But at least at Christmas we do know that there *is* another sense of values in which true worth lies. If the magic which possesses us at Christmas could only be made to last, how different the world picture would look. It is a world in which all men want peace—and prepare for war; a world in which there is plenty for all to eat, and yet where millions perish with hunger. In a world which might be as bright as a Spring morning, our hates and fears and suspicions make a bitter winter, heartless and cold as death.

When the Christ Child draws our stubborn necks as low as His manger, and when His spirit really rules our hearts, only then can the New Age be born and the Christmas magic last for ever.

The Anchorage of Our Faith

No one can deny that the sea of religious thought in this country is heaving with unrest, and the minds of many are disquieted. At such a time it is a good thing to contemplate one's anchorage. My own mind is steadied when I meditate how its security may be realized.

One chain that holds the anchor is the indubitable arrival of Christ in history. I shall never forget the warm sense of reassurance which came into my heart when I visited Bethlehem over thirty years ago and heard the guide say, "Jesus Christ was born here." Take away as legend, if you will, the stories of wise men following a star, of shepherds surprised by a heavenly host, and even an angel's visit to a virgin girl.

Nevertheless, while some religions had their entire origins in myths, this religion began with the birth of a man, as pagan historians agree, who lived in places one can still visit, who died a terrible death, and who, by a method as yet not understood, so convinced His followers of His survival, that eleven runaways became preachers of His gospel, beginning at the very place where, if their story had been refutable, they could have been made a laughing-stock, and silenced for ever.

Another chain that secures the anchor for me is the strange

fact that we are still discussing who He was, as well as what He said and did. A Figure which *can* be dismissed does not remain a live issue in men's thoughts for two thousand years. Was He a man? Indubitably, but to pile all the evidence about Him upon the frail craft called "human" makes it sink. It cannot carry all that cargo. Shall we say He was "divine"? I have to do so, because the only other vessel to carry the evidence has capsized, but I don't know what the word means, He was poor and lonely, forsaken and tortured, and He let Himself be put to death. Yet the words of this executed "criminal" have been translated into every known language, His life illumines both the word "human" and the word "divine", and His standard of loving has enthralled the imaginations of men in every race under Heaven. When He has been followed, men's lives have been changed, and more people love Him today than ever before in history.

The third chain that holds my anchor is my own experience. I am a Scot, and we are a reticent folk. But as a boy of nine I made my little act of dedication to Christ one New Year's Sunday and wrote down the fact in a diary someone had given me for Christmas. Needless to say, I have gone back on that vow a thousand times, but still He holds my heart in thrall. I know no peace of mind outside His will, and no joy like that released by trying to do it.

No storm can make an anchor drag if it is held by such strong chains.

Guiding Hands

On Palm Sunday throughout all Christendom people hear again the story of a Messiah riding in so-called triumph into the capital. Like so many other deeds of Jesus it was an acted parable carefully arranged beforehand, so that none who knew the Scriptures could miss its message. "Rejoice greatly, O daughter of Zion," the prophet Zechariah had sung, "Behold, thy King cometh unto thee: He is just, and having salvation; lowly and riding upon an ass."

IT WAS an admission of Messiahship and has been called a "triumphal entry", but it was a triumph that turned to tears. For when the road uphill turned the shoulder of the Mount of Olives and the gleaming turrets of Jerusalem with the golden dome of the temple burst into view, Jesus could bear the play-acting no longer. "When He drew nigh He saw the city and *broke down in sobs*." (The Greek word is much stronger than the word for "weeping" used in the story of His weeping at the death of Lazarus.) "If thou hadst known," He cried, "the things which belong unto peace, but now they are hid from thine eyes."

How relevant is the story for our times! How ardently we slave for the things that peace brings! How dilatory we are to discipline ourselves to produce the things that bring peace: things like love and unselfishness and tolerance and brotherliness!

The individual often feels he can do but little. But every one of us could submit himself to the will of Christ as he understands it at each moment.

THIRTY years ago I heard a true story about a cowboy, who having listened to the Palm Sunday narrative said, "What wonderful hands Jesus must have had!" "Why do you say that?" his friends asked. "Well," said the cowboy, "a man who can sit on an unbroken colt on which no one has ever sat before, and master it, and guide it, and soothe it when

118

people are crowding round it shrieking 'Hosanna' in its ears, waving palms before its eyes, and throwing clothes in front of its feet, that man must have wonderful hands."

At least we can submit our mulish, undisciplined wills to His guiding hands. Surely we have failed often enough by ourselves to let Him take over the control.

The Meaning of Christ's Cross Today

DURING Lent, many give a little time to meditation on the meaning of Christ's death. Many thoughtful young people find that some of the older theories about it do not offer them a place where their minds can rest satisfied. They cannot believe that a brutal murder was the will of God. Nor can they find much truth in theories which put God on a judge's bench and Christ in the dock paying the penalty of the world's sin.

"How," they ask, "can sin be 'paid for' thus?" We forgive our children without exacting a "price" in terms of suffering. Couldn't God do the same, and didn't the Old Testament saints find forgiveness before Christ's death took place? Isn't it a fiction to sing, "I lay my sins on Jesus" when every psychologist knows that one thing that cannot be transferred from one person to another is guilt, and that sin cannot be paid for as one pays a debt? And what has His death so long ago to do with my sins today?

QUESTIONS multiply, and though the thinkers of every age have every right to explore mystery by the use of current thought forms, as for instance St. Paul did, we must be allowed to do the same. No use of words can banish mystery, but for myself I found some light in remembering that any man, to the extent to which he is good, is revealing the nature of God. It seems to me that Christ, by being willing to go to the uttermost length to demonstrate love in action— and no man, while still in the flesh, can do more than die— reveals the nature of God and His attitude to sin, namely to go on loving endlessly, whatever men do, until men wake up to see what sin costs God and, yielding at last to love, allow it to change them.

I remember one night in the Mediterranean we passed quite close to Stromboli, an island volcano which rises sheer out of the sea. It was after dinner and almost dark. Suddenly there was a great burst of flame from the crater at the summit. Huge tongues of flame shot up hundreds of feet into the sky, lighting up the ocean for miles around. Tons of molten rock were thrown up into the air. Through our glasses it was possible to distinguish red-hot boulders racing down the mountain-side, and gradually a stream of lava forced its way almost to the sea. For some hours—when our vessel had slipped westwards towards the last lingering light of sunset which lay upon the horizon; when the bold outline of Stromboli was lost in the gathering shadows of night— that red-hot stream of lava, like some awful, open wound, gashed the darkness. What did it mean? It meant that for a few hours there had been revealed those great fires which had been burning in the mountain's heart since the foundation of the world.

> I sometimes think about the Cross,
>   And shut my eyes and try to see
> The cruel nails and crown of thorns,
>   And Jesus, crucified for me.

But even could I see Him die,
    I could but see a little part
Of that great love, which like a fire,
    Is *always* burning in His heart.

It seems to me that that Love is the final meaning of the universe, the message of the Cross and the only hope of the world.

The Price of Sin

AT Easter we sing, "There was no other good enough to pay the price of sin", but we must never imagine a kind of balance sheet in which the physical sufferings of Christ cancel and "pay for" the sin of mankind. Sin cannot thus be dealt with. Words like "propitiation", "sacrifice", "oblation", "satisfaction", used in some services, can terribly mislead.

God did not need to have His anger bought off (propitiated) by the suffering of the innocent Christ, nor was Christ's death a sacrifice by substitution in the way the Jews sacrificed a lamb. Christ offered Himself to God as an oblation, but not in the Jewish sense, nor did God need "satisfaction" in the sense of one who says of human sin, "Someone must pay for this or I cannot forgive without losing face."

Christ pays "the price of sin" inasmuch as He identifies Himself with us. One thinks of Quisling, the dastardly traitor. If his wife loved him and stuck to him and went on wearing his name, she would "pay the price of sin" by her loving identification. Christ's self-giving on the Cross was both a revelation and a pledge. A revelation of love's willingness to go to the uttermost and a pledge that He, who is still human and one of us, will always bear our name and nature and stand by us until we are changed. This is at-one-ment.

But, of course, the sinner also pays "the price of sin" and can never evade this tax! It is in two parts, penalty and consequence. The penalty is separation from God and consequent deterioration of character. This penalty is cancelled by our sincere penitence and God's forgiveness. The soul's *relationship* with God is restored as though sin had never broken it. But the consequences of sin are not abolished by forgiveness, for we live in a world of cause and effect. These consequences may affect body, mind or spirit, or all three. While forgiveness does not abolish consequence it changes its nature from being a Nemesis in an impersonal world of cause and effect, to being a discipline accepted willingly, since by it the soul achieves a deepening harmony with God.

The Nature of Sacrifice

On Passion Sunday we think of the sacrifice of Christ. It seems important to relinquish the ancient Jewish idea of sacrifice which contained elements alien to modern thought in the West. The Jew offered a lamb on an altar, identified himself with it, and regarded the sacrifice as a means of obtaining forgiveness. So, when Jesus was killed, it seemed to the Jew that here was the climax of centuries of "sin-offerings". Was He not the Lamb of God slain for the sins of the world?

The danger is that such language pictures God as an angry

Deity whose wrath can only be bought off by someone paying, in terms of physical agony, what is called "the price of sin". The truth is that "God was in Christ", one with Him in intention, in action and in reaction.

Alas! the heresy has got into our Communion Service where we talk of "sacrifice, oblation, satisfaction and propitiation" as though a loving Father could not forgive His penitent children unless someone suffered a mythical equivalent of pain to buy off His wrath. What a fiend a god would be who demanded such "satisfaction"!

The heresy is also in our hymn books. After a reference to the "blood of beasts on Jewish altars slain", we sing that "Christ, the heavenly Lamb, takes all our sins away; A sacrifice of nobler name and richer blood than they". There is nothing in the Gospels to justify this view of sacrifice. The Father, in the Prodigal story (Luke 15), ran out to meet the returning penitent and restored him at once. He didn't have to be "propitiated", or "satisfied" by yet more pain. Everyone who loves a sinner pays "the price of sin" in terms of his loving identification, but the Jewish idea is definitely out. Christ never called Himself the Lamb of God.

Even the mystery religions, which powerfully influenced early Christian thought, still throw their shadow over us. In the ceremony of the taurobolium, a penitent in a pit was literally washed in the blood of an animal slaughtered on a lattice above his head. So we still talk of being "washed in blood" and sing:

> There is a fountain filled with blood,
>   Drawn from Immanuel's veins;
> And sinners plunged beneath that flood,
>   Lose all their guilty stains.

Is it not time we escaped from this revolting imagery and

saw Christ's sacrifice as certainly more exacting than words can express, but made as joyfully as that of a woman who, in giving birth to a child, abandons social delights and goes through agony with joy because a man is born into the world?

The Incredible Certainty

ONE of the fundamentals of the Christian Faith is, to the modern, one of its greatest difficulties. The fundamental is that Jesus Christ survived death and proved His survival to His followers, changing them overnight from fugitive cowards to missionary martyrs.

Those who read thrillers are aware of the difficulty of disposing of a body, and we may be sure that if Christ's enemies had hidden it they would have produced it and murdered Christianity as well as Christ. If His friends had hidden it they would have venerated it. They certainly would not have made an empty tomb the basis of a message for which they were willing to die. All possibilities have been explored, but we are left with an empty tomb and with grave-clothes in a position which suggested that He had "passed through the body" and assumed a different means of manifestation, a means which made on the senses of those who loved Him the same mental impression as a physical body had made, together with evidence of other powers—such as passing through closed doors—which had not earlier been His.

For myself I am convinced that future discoveries in the field of psychic research, which man will make when he examines that field with all the scientific disciplines now used in, say, physics, will illumine for us the manner of the

Resurrection. Probably before Christ died, He who revealed such amazing power over other men's bodies set in motion energies in regard to His own which culminated in His finishing finally with matter as we know it and emerging from the tomb in a "body" of a different vibration altogether.

But the manner is less important than the fact. No one doubts that Hannibal crossed the Alps, even though Livy and Polybus, the two chief historians, give completely irreconcilable accounts of it.

For the Christian, the enheartening truth is that Christ defeated man's last enemy and still lives, the conqueror over pain and sin and death. This leads the Christian to believe that evil does not have the last word for him either, and that he will find unspeakable joy at the end of his journey with all that seems hostile to love woven into a plan greater than his present power to perceive.

Once the sun has risen no hand can pluck it from the sky, even though man's smoke may obscure its shining.

> Whatever clouds may veil the sky
> Never is night again.

The Resurrection of Christ

Recently a theory has been repeated, which Renan put forward long ago, that Jesus did not actually die on the Cross but fainted, revived in the tomb, and continued His ministry. Thus we are relieved of the strain of believing in the Resurrection!

But the "explanation" leaves too many questions unanswered. Would a teacher who had prophesied his resurrection pretend to his men that he had risen if he had never died? How could a man, so weak that he could not carry his own cross, who had been scourged, tortured, nailed by hands and feet to a cross, left there for hours through a hot day, wounded with a spear thrust, bound in grave clothes and shut in a cave-tomb, get off a stone slab, remove the tightly wound wrappings, push back a heavy stone which it took several soldiers to move, evade the guards, procure other clothing, and then join his friends, not as an invalid needing weeks of nursing, but as a man fit enough to walk on wounded feet fourteen miles—to Emmaus and back (Luke 24: 13 ff.)—before joining his friends at supper at Jerusalem?

This theory only postpones another question. When *did* Jesus die, and what happened to His body *then*? Those most concerned were either enemies or friends. Enemies, finding the body, would have exposed the Resurrection story at once. Friends would have buried the body and venerated the tomb. They would not have preached the Resurrection within six weeks of the crucifixion in the very neighbourhood where it happened, nor would the eleven have finally died for a lie.

A more likely theory, which further psychic research may illumine, is that Christ, whose healing miracles showed amazing power over the matter of other men's bodies, had a unique power over His own. In some way, as yet unexplained, but not unimagined, He may have effected a dematerialization of the matter of His body, and found subsequent expression in an etheric body, which, after His burial, made a similar impression on the senses of His followers as His physical presence made before it.

The supreme truth is that the essential Christ survived death, proved His survival to His followers, and is for ever available, though unseen, to those who seek Him.

THE THINGS WHICH REMAIN

The Real Thing

IN MOST areas of life we distinguish between the counterfeit and the real thing, for instance, paste and diamonds. In religion we seem unaware that the Church is immeasurably weakened by counterfeit Christianity.

When we think of the religion of Christ which swept through the known world, though its apostles had no money for advertising and organizing, no social status or prestige, and little education, we must be bewildered by our slow advance. A modern church service often has in support glorious architecture, first-class music, educated teaching and also the official backing of the State. Yet the impact it makes is so small that if eight out of ten churches were closed the community would hardly notice the difference.

The impact on the community was greater when the Church was persecuted by the State, and had no artistic adjuncts, but had a burning message of redemption, a vivid personal experience of spiritual power, and a fellowship which possessed and shared such a quality of life, such a mastery of the art of living, such an infectious gaiety and inward serenity, that others who watched sought to find out the secret.

IT WOULD be valuable, though searching, to ask ourselves,

and honestly answer, some personal questions: If all the early Christians had been like me, how far would Christianity have spread? Or this: Have I really got anything from my religion worth passing on to another? Or this: When people see my life does it make them want something that I've got from my Christian experience or do they only see a dull fake, an unattractive substitute for the real thing? Or this: Could I answer from my own experience the age-long question of a soul who confided in me, crying, "O that I knew where I might find Him"?

Reality in Christian experience, could, I think, be assessed by noting three facts about the real Christian:

1. The real Christian tries to react in every important decision and crisis in the spirit he has observed in Christ. All real Christians do not necessarily believe the same thing or worship in the same way, but none would act in any situation in an un-Christlike way.

2. The real Christian senses that in finding Christ he is only at the end of his wandering, not at the end of his journey. There is always more to find and he may be in another world before he has found the pearl of great price for which he is searching: before he can really say the General Thanksgiving with complete sincerity, thanking God more for Christ than for "all the blessings of this life".

3. The real Christian sincerely wants others to possess what he has found in religion: power, guidance, meaningfulness and purposefulness. We are all very shy about our religious experience and we must never burgle another's soul. But equally we cannot be content with a kind of private salvation. Indeed, it goes bad on us.

Many need assurances about religion. Those who possess the real thing *are* assurances of religion. As Alfred Noyes said, "Anyone who doubts the validity and reality of

Christian experience should see my father's face as he returns from Holy Communion."

The Simple Gospel

Amid all the multitude of books on religion, the differences among the denominations, the formulated creeds and the discussions in factories, colleges and schools, it may be of some value if someone tries to say in a few hundred words what to him is the essence of the Gospel, though it can only be an individual's point of view, and over-simplified at that.

In seven words my summary of the Gospel is this: God offers us His friendship in Christ. When we turn back to the beginning we see Jesus calling men to enter His fellowship. He made no demand on them to believe theological propositions. "Follow Me" was the invitation which they accepted. When they watched Him and listened and meditated, they must have said in their hearts, "This is what God meant human life to be like." They noted His compassion for others, His belief in God's love, His faith in them, His joy and gaiety and His inward serenity. His was a transforming friendship, and gradually, within His fellowship, they were changed men. His love flowed through them to others. They could get on with one another, and they felt—as many of us still feel—that His vision of the Kingdom of right relationships with God and with man, which He called the Kingdom of Heaven, is the key for which the whole world is groping and the way to end all our sorrows.

When He was put to death, they never regarded it as an execution by others, but rather as a self-giving on His part, which, more clearly than ever, showed them the ways of love. If He, who could so easily have escaped, would die rather than give up loving, then God, of whom He was their picture, would also go to *His* uttermost and never forsake them. Christ's resurrection, however hard to understand, proved for them that nothing can destroy love, and that in the Unseen He was committed to them, and to all men, for ever. His death was both a revelation and a pledge that man is in the hands of a Love which will never let him off, never let him down, and never let him go.

For myself, conversion was rather like falling in love. In regard to the latter, I found someone whose life I wanted to share and whom I wanted to have share my life. What I believed about her grew out of my experience with her, as did the true "apostles' creed" in regard to Christ. To impose a creed first as a condition of fellowship is hopelessly wrong both in love and in religion. I would accept, for church membership, anyone who wanted to try out Christ's way of life, whatever he believed and whatever he had done, and I would define a Christian as one who tried to meet life's demands and challenges in the spirit of Jesus Christ as far as he could discern it, and who tried to spread that spirit in the world.

Here then is the A.B.C. of Christianity. Admit your need. Believe that Christ can meet it, since He has done so for millions. Commit yourself to Him. He will do the rest if you keep close.

On Eternal Punishment

I AM glad that a correspondent challenged the idea, still current among some churchpeople, of eternal punishment. Surely the time has come when we must throw over, and dismiss finally from our minds, the vulgar superstition that anyone, whatever he believes or does, is landed in some kind of endless torture after death. How can we believe that God would stoop to an unjust piece of cruelty for which a man would be despised? A man, for far less, would be deemed a fiend, and sent to gaol or to a criminal lunatic asylum.

It is worth noting that no word is used in the Gospels which could be translated "endless". "Agelong", or "aeonian", perhaps, but not "endless".

THE GOSPEL writers, like our own grandfathers, distorted the message of Jesus, impelled to do so by that streak of malice in human nature which would torture those who disagree. Even the disciples wanted to call down fire from heaven merely because certain Samaritans would not invite them to supper! (Luke 9: 54, N.E.B.)

But the distortion of the imagery of fire does not mean that we can dismiss it. I know my own heart well enough to know that there is much to be "burned away" before I can be made fit for complete communion with God. The incident of dying makes no one a saint. We go on where we left off, though, let us hope, with clearer vision about the worthwhile values, and a desire for, not a resentment against, whatever discipline God ordains for our further development.

One last thought. There can be no heaven for anyone if a single soul languishes in hell. Could even we, let alone God, enjoy bliss while one soul was excluded from it? I believe in a Good Shepherd who will never close the door of the sheepfold while there is one sheep lost in the wilderness of estrangement, but who will seek it with all the ardour of endless love, *until He finds it*. (Luke 15:4)

Strength from the Forward Look

How one admires those who tread a pathway of steadfast purpose until they achieve their goal, finding strength for the present in their vision of the future.

A lot of pious nonsense is talked about ambition. To "get on" by pushing others down, or by using methods which, in old age, will be regretted bitterly, is wrong. But to mobilize all one's powers and draft them into front-line service is to store up contentment, instead of frustration, for life's eventide.

Man is a trinity of thinking, willing and feeling.

1. *The light that steadies his thinking is truth*. Truths can be *imposed* upon man and his assent obtained, but the only truths which will be of any value in a crisis are those which authenticate themselves in his own mind. One can only *believe* what one sees to be true. Belief, different from assent, can never be imposed by outward authority, however august. One gathers intellectual strength by one's forward-

looking search for self-authenticating truth, not by trying to swallow ideas which others say are true.

2. *The light that steadies man's willing is duty.* Again and again, one gathers strength for the dull stretches of the road by simply doing the next task which duty demands. When God seems distant, prayer futile, and when life seems to have no purpose, meaning or beauty; when we feel lonely, insignificant and defeated, we can offer our wills to God and just do the next job. This offering is of equal value to Him as are the ecstasies of emotional hallelujahs. To set before ourselves the goal of duty is to draw strength for dull days.

3. *The light that steadies our feeling is loving commitment.* He who gives love obtains love. A marriage is sustained through all life's irritations and disappointments because there is an underlying commitment of the one to the other, and one, or ideally both, are determined to make the marriage a success. The vision of the goal ahead gives a strength that carries determined lovers through difficult moments or even years.

Jesus said we must love God with all our heart (feeling), strength (will) and mind (intellect). When all three are directed toward a goal set before us we gather strength from the forward look.

Strength from the Backward Look

WE ARE constantly exhorted to look forward and to put the past behind us, but sometimes it is strengthening and comforting to look back. Memory can gather light from the past and shed it on the present and the future.

1. I believe that God guides men, but, for myself, it is only when I look back that I am sure. At the cross-roads I have often been puzzled, and, lacking any sense of guidance, have mistakenly thought that I was left to find my own way.

2. I believe in God's providence, but when I look *back* I see that what He provided was never immunity from the ills and accidents which beset others, but an assurance that He was sharing and caring *in* every experience, and offering me in it a creative opportunity, a right response to which would lead to spiritual gain.

I shiver when I hear the successful and complacent say, "God has been very good to me," lest they suppose He has been less good to a cancer patient or to a bereaved mother. God's providence, like the rain and sunlight, falls impartially on all (Matthew 5: 45) and it is only when we stop equating providence with the receipt of the things we call "good" that we can see that God can work with equal final success through the things we call "evil". As I look *back*, I can see that God has done as much good with the things I labelled "evil" as with the things I called "good", and which I was tempted to regard as alone the tokens of "providence". He did more with Christ's cross than with the lilies Christ praised as illustrations of God's providence. This does not justify evil, but it demonstrates that evil can be made the occasion of final good, (Psalm 76: 10.) and this is the only excuse God has for permitting it.

3. I believe that God is ever near, but I can only reassure myself about this by looking back on past experiences when His presence was indubitable. So, when He seems far away I tell myself that there *have* been occasions when I have been certain of His presence, and that since *He* never varies, it must be some dark mood in me, or some variation in health or fatigue, which is dimming my awareness of Him.

136

Let us then look back to even one moment of certainty about God, and then realize that *always* "in Him we live and move and have our being".

Inner Certainty

Rᴇʟɪɢɪᴏᴜs experience is a strange and elusive thing. I can quite understand those for whom the phrase means nothing. I also know that one cannot engineer religious experience. No amount of attendance at religious services, making one's communion, engaging in private prayer or reading religious books will guarantee the kind of experience that made the young Isaiah cry, "Woe is me! . . . for mine eyes have seen the King, the Lord of Hosts," or made Peter the simple fisherman cry, "Depart from me, for I am a sinful man, O Lord."

When that strange, awesome sense of the numinous *does* fall upon the spirit, it is far more compelling and convincing about the reality of God's existence than are any intellectual arguments, valuable though these may be. It is as though one glimpsed on a Swiss holiday, for only a few moments, the shining, snow-clad peaks. Days of rain and mist may follow and the weather make the view as depressing as Bloomsbury in a November fog. But *one knows the peaks are there*. And no arguments could make one deny that they had been seen. There is an inner certainty based on experience and nothing can destroy it.

In a ministry of over fifty years, there have only been half a dozen occasions when I have experienced this "tremendous mystery". The rest is a matter of plodding through the mist by dogged obedience rather than by glowing vision, a plodding often broken by acts of disobedience and darkened by days of cold indifference. *But I know the peaks of reality are there.*

AND although we cannot engineer and arrange to have a spiritual experience, since the "wind bloweth where it listeth", we can at least put the sail up. In *Signs in the Storm*, Joseph Nemes tells how he was beaten up by the Russians and was expecting death. He turned to the sixteenth chapter of St. Matthew's Gospel and began to read. "As I was doing this," he says, "all of a sudden light came to me. It was as if a very important message had been flashed to me from another world, and this light made it easy for me to find the way out victoriously."

Scores of writers, not just the saints, speak of this kind of experience. C. S. Lewis is "surprised by joy". Sidney Royse Lysaght saw "Visions too beautiful to be untrue". Winifred Holtby on a hillside sensed a reality that made a fatal illness unimportant. Milton knew a "moment of enormous bliss". John Buchan tells of a moment when he "seemed to be a happy part of a friendly universe". Rupert Brooke had a significant "hour of knowing". C. F. Andrews wrote, "A veil seemed lifted from my eyes and the whole world was wrapped in inexpressible glory". William de Morgan saw the shining peaks as he listened to a symphony of Beethoven and wrote, "If reality is like that, I have no cause to be anxious or afraid".

It *is* like that. For us now, the plodding in the mist, with only the occasional glimpse to cheer us. But at last the sunlit heights for ever!

Is Hell Endless?

I⊤ IS interesting to find that this question arises whenever questions about Christianity are invited. Two mistakes are commonly made. One is to suppose that Our Lord painted the vulgar picture of unending torture which misguided preachers painted a hundred years ago. Unending *punishment* is a contradiction in terms, for the end of punishment is reformation. If the *punishment* is unending, when does the victim show the benefit he has gained? If Hell is endless, it is valueless.

Jesus based this figure of speech on the fires that devoured rubbish thrown into the valley of Hinnom near Jerusalem. The fire went on burning so long as there was anything left which flame could consume. The remainder and the ashes were used to make roads. Much in our character needs to be purged, but there is an indestructible residue which contains eternal values both personal and social.

The other mistake is to erase from our minds all thought of Hell; to suppose that it represents a superstition which we can now dismiss as the outmoded thinking of an earlier age. But it should be remembered that, although our grandfathers caricatured Hell and made it the work of a fiend, its origin lies in the authentic words of Jesus. He used the most compassionate, loving and tolerant words about sinners which have ever been spoken, but He used the most terrible words about sin which human ears have ever heard. And He was no fanatic who got wildly excited about things which matter little. It was *Jesus* who talked about the shut door and age-long flame, the outer darkness full of weeping. At the end of the most tender of all His parables, we find words like this: "My son was *dead* and is alive again; he was *lost* and is found." "Dead!" "Lost!" That is what Christ thinks of what sin can do to us. A man would emasculate Christianity who took out of it Christ's teaching that un-repented sin brings consequences which are terrible indeed.

I remember hearing about a man who dreamed that he went to heaven and was greatly delighted with all he was shown. Then the angelic guide asked him if he would like to visit Hell. He said he would, but he soon cried out that he could see nothing because of the heat and blaze of the flames. "Can you *hear* nothing?" asked the guide. To his surprise the dreamer heard the strange and beautiful music of many voices coming from the heart of the fire. "Sir," said the dreamer to his guide, "tell me what are those wondrous songs which the souls in Hell itself are singing?" The angelic guide whispered in his ear. "They are the songs of the redeemed," he said.

The Day of Judgment

The day I enter an art gallery is for me a day of judgment. No court is necessary; neither is any voice of approval or condemnation. The pictures themselves judge me, and, unless I pretend, I am forced to accept their verdict. When a tourist visited a famous art gallery and spoke slightingly of the pictures to an attendant, the latter replied significantly, "Sir, the *pictures* are not on trial!"

The day I attend a concert of classical music perfectly

played is for me a day of judgment. Either I appreciate the music or I am bored. Even the magic name Beethoven cannot *make* me enjoy the music. And I need no judge or jury or staged trial or uttered verdict. The music itself judges me as to whether I love music or not. The verdict—unless I can lie even to myself—is inescapable.

Some religious writers have talked of a "day of judgment" and painted a grim picture of an assize with a Divine Judge on a throne and a trembling sinner awaiting a verdict which means either heaven or hell. They have based this on one single chapter in St. Matthew's Gospel (25) which scholars tell us he borrowed from the apochryphal book of Enoch, and which in any case is a parable about nations not individuals.

Of the individual, Jesus said, "I judge him not: for I came not to judge the world but to save the world . . . the word that I spake, the same shall judge him in that day." And any day when I am confronted by spiritual reality is a judgment day and my reaction to that reality expresses the verdict inescapably.

SURELY the day on which I slip away from this material world into one in which spiritual values are as important as music at a concert, will be a day of judgment. Spiritual realities will themselves judge me. It will be little use then wishing that I hadn't thought so highly of money, fame, power, success, social position, dress, pleasure or sex, and so little of love, compassion and service, nor will it be much good telling the angel who looks after me that I was once a churchwarden, or at one time intended being a missionary, or had an aunt who was a big Baptist!

To a lover of music a perfect concert is a bit of heaven, but it could be as boring as hell to one incapable of making any inner response to its loveliness. Perhaps that is what hell is; an incapability of responding to spiritual loveliness brought on by a complete disregard of spiritual reality here.

BUT for some, the day of judgment at death will be the happiest day of their lives. For one thing, all the evidence shows that dying is a beautiful experience. For another, they will feel for the first time completely understood. All the secret battles they have fought for goodness, and all the longings for holiness will be seen to have been so worthwhile. And, though painful, how blessed it will be to have all the façades down, all pretence ended, all excuses finished, all evasions seen through, and not to have to hide anything any more!

The Things Which Remain

FEW young people, I imagine, have read these articles. Today, at any rate, I write for those in the second half of life. Such achievement as may have been ours, lies in the past. We can never, we feel, do or be some of the things on which we set our youthful hearts, nor any longer cherish high hopes, make new resolutions or register noble vows.

First of all, for our encouragement, let me reel off some biographical facts. Beethoven was forty-five when he wrote the Seventh and Eighth symphonies and fifty-two when he wrote the Ninth. Julius Caesar's fame is that of a great military leader but he was forty-nine before he became a soldier. Sir Winston Churchill was over fifty when he started to paint, and Tennyson began to paint at seventy. Morley's life of Gladstone in three volumes shows that two out of the three concern his life after fifty. Darwin wrote his greatest work when over sixty. Verdi wrote his two finest operas at age seventy-three and eighty. John Wesley was writing new sermons and preaching them at four in the morning when he was eighty-six. Cato learnt Greek at eighty, and Titian painted in his hundredth year. On my shelves is a book, written by a physician, entitled "How to be Useful and Happy from 60–90"! So let us take heart: "Some work of noble note may yet be done."

Ours is a world sick and tired of words, but hungry for deeds. One might well endeavour each day to make someone's heart lighter, someone's path easier. It is better, we have been told, to light one small candle than to curse the darkness, and there are few of us, whatever our age or our assessment of our own inability to do anything for the world, who could not write a letter of cheer, speak a word of encouragement, call on some lonely soul, enhearten the discouraged, or tell a funny story to someone treading a sad path.

Apart from day-to-day activities, however, all of us in the second half of life would do well to ask what life is all about.

In my view this life is the lowest form in God's school. We pass on to the next, and the next, in order to be trained ultimately to enjoy fellowship with Him and to be all that He can make us. Death is only passing into another form in God's school, but it would be wise, especially in the second half of life, to prepare for it. We shall put down the body with all its lusts and desires. Money and possessions, social status and academic distinction are all left behind.

There are things which remain. We shall take our power to love and serve, our knowledge of true values, our

143

sensitivity to beauty and, I hope, our sense of humour. Above all we shall take, what everyone has deep down, a longing for high and noble things.

For myself, I don't want to go back and be young again. It is better further on. In the meantime let us deserve that most beautiful of all epitaphs: "When we saw the glory of his sunset, we said, 'It will be a lovely day tomorrow'."